Reconstructing the past

Alan Sorrell

Reconstructing the past

Edited by
Mark Sorrell

Book Club Associates   London

Acknowledgment

Mark Sorrell would like especially to thank the National Museum of Wales for their generous assistance in the preparation of this book.

Thanks are also expressed to the following for their kind permission to reproduce copyright illustrations:

Leslie Alcock Esq., for the drawing on page 113;

Anglia Television, for the drawing on pages 118–9;

The Trustees of the British Museum, for the drawing on page 36;

The Castle Museum, Shrewsbury, for the drawing on pages 84–5 and colour plate 1;

City of London Police Headquarters, for the drawings on pages 54–5, 58–9;

Coventry Museum, for the drawings on pages 41, 42, 43;

Department of the Environment (Crown Copyright—reproduced with permission of the Controller of Her Majesty's Stationery Office), for the drawings on pages 29, 30, 31, 34 (bottom), 46 (top), 46 (bottom), 47, 49, 50, 52, 79, 81, 88, 105, 107, 114, 115, 116, 121, 122, 124, 127, 133, 134, 136, 138, 139, 141, 143, 144, 146, 148, 154, 156–7, 158, 160, 162, 164 and colour plates 3 and 4;

Dorset County Museum (Dorset Natural History and Archaeological Society), for the drawing on page 39;

The Illustrated London News, for the drawings on pages 27, 44, 66, 96, 99, 102, 109;

The Museum of London, for the drawings on pages 37, 56, 60, 61, 62, 64, 67, 68;

The National Museum of Wales, for the drawings on pages 87, 91;

Norfolk Museums Service (Norwich Castle Museum), for the drawing on page 104;

Scottish Development Department (Crown Copyright), for the drawings on pages 94, 95, 97, 129, 131, 149, 151, 153;

F. D. Todman Esq., for the drawing on page 110;

The Verulamium Museum, St Albans, for the drawings on pages 70, 72, 74–5, 77;

Worthing Museum, for the drawing on pages 112–3.

This edition published 1981
by Book Club Associates
by arrangement with
Batsford Academic
and Educational Ltd,
4 Fitzhardinge Street, London W1H 0AH

ISBN 0 7134 1588 6

Contents

Foreword

By Professor B. W. Cunliffe

Archaeology has been particularly fortunate in being able to attract the services of a man like Alan Sorrell though service is perhaps too stark a word for the loving care which he lavished on each and every one of his brilliant reconstructions. To those of us whose interests were kindled and nurtured by the remarkable wave of popular archaeology in the 1950s the name of Alan Sorrell was as well known as those of Glyn Daniel and Sir Mortimer Wheeler. All were experts and scholars in their own fields and all were using their powers of communication to breathe life into the unprepossessing rubble foundations and dreary potsherds that formed the raw material of archaeological research.

Alan Sorrell's particular genius lay in his ability to visualize in three dimensions. The buildings which rose up from ground-plans in meticulously researched detail were made to work as structures. Materials were as correct as the evidence would allow, the roof lines were carefully considered and all the stresses and strains of a real structure were taken into account. A Sorrell building not only looked as though it could stand, one could confidently believe that it had stood! But these were not clinical architectural drawings, they were part of a living landscape, sometimes raw with squalls sweeping across threatening skies, sometimes busy with activity but always gripped with a tense energy—a swirling flock of sheep at Heathrow, tortured branches of dead trees at Llantwit Major—you can feel the mire underfoot and smell the lichen.

The high viewpoint which he so frequently adopted is particularly successful. By rising slightly, entire building complexes could be brought into view, roofs could be shown in their complex articulation and the countryside setting spread out before us. If greater attention needed to be focused on a single structure or if a building's surroundings were unknown the eye-line could be dropped accordingly. Compare, for example, Conway Castle and Harlech Castle (pp. 138–9): by careful adjustment of viewpoint the irrelevant is omitted, repetition of un-necessary detail is avoided, while the siting of each castle is brilliantly portrayed.

In a Sorrell drawing there are no glib answers, nothing results from the easy way out. How well the working drawings express the meticulous nature of the research. Those of us who have had the pleasure of working with him will remember, above all, this care for detail—a meeting to discuss the nature of the problems, the first working sketches, the questions and the problems. We were all made to think hard and (certainly in my case) to learn something new of the building we thought we knew. Nothing was left to chance—the last communication I received about a reconstruction of the temple at Bath was a postcard asking if I had a picture of the modern sky line looking south, otherwise he would have to go to Bath to do his own sketch!

Alan Sorrell's drawings have been an inspiration to amateur enthusiasts and professional archaeologists alike. Their accuracy, their timeless quality and the fact that they are works of art in their own right will ensure that they continue to inspire for generations to come.

B. W. Cunliffe
Institute of Archaeology
Oxford

16 December 1980

Introduction

Alan Sorrell was born at Tooting in south London in 1904. When he was two years old, the family moved to the seaside town of Southend in Essex. His father, who was a master jeweller and watch-maker, and in his leisure time a keen amateur painter, died suddenly in 1910.

From his earliest years, Alan Sorrell showed a passion for drawing and painting and, somewhat against the wishes of his family, who had other plans for him, persevered in his ambition to become a painter. He began his training at the Southend Municipal School of Art in 1919, and after four years' study, and a further year in the City supporting himself as a commercial designer, was admitted to the Royal College of Art in 1924. In 1928, he won the Prix de Rome in painting with a composition of allegorical figures for a wall-decoration, entitled 'People seeking after Wisdom'.

The scholarship took him to the British School at Rome for two years. He has left a very funny account of his time there, and is unsparing in his portrait of an earnest, rather timid young man with his 'small trades-man's' attitudes, Non-conformist prejudices, and long-pondered theories of art. In Italy he had what every artist needs, time to search and study and think, with the stimulus of contact with scholars of other disciplines. The note of facetious self-deprecation is insistent, but he was as yet struggling to find his way.

He returned to England in 1931 with a new confidence, keenly antici-pating the schemes of mural decoration he would be called upon to undertake, and with visions of vast wall-spaces to be filled, in town halls and Parliament buildings. Sir William Rothenstein, the Principal of the College, who had always been very kind and interested in his work, offered him a post on the teaching staff of the College, as an instructor of drawing, which relieved him of some present anxieties. Turning again to the consideration of painting 'jobs', he now bethought him of his home town of Southend, and more particularly of the Municipal Library, with its walls of 'bluish-white' plaster, as a suitable candidate. He approached the Mayor of Southend, and with gratifying ease, secured the com-mission of four large panels. The chosen subjects were to be 'history book themes', which was rather a disappointment to this young artist, who had planned a series of 'genuine historical paintings of the only history we can know—that of our own time', but his gratitude overrode his disap-pointment.

The first subject was to be the 'Refitting of Admiral Blake's Fleet at Leigh' in 1652, 2.74 metres by 1.22 metres. How was this to be tackled? He consoled himself that the subject did not really matter: 'Fine shape and colour is possible whether you deal with Admiral Blake or apples on a plate: the only disadvantage of dealing with unfamiliar shapes and scenes is that you cannot understand them so well, or consider them as intimately, as you would everyday things'. The first task of the artist who does not know his subject, he concluded, must be to learn it before he can properly paint it, 'with an intense study of each object, each square yard of land, sea and sky, and then perhaps, when your pencil goes to paper, or your brush to the canvas, it will be handled with, at any rate, some degree of certainty and conviction'.

Fortunately, although the period and incidents of the proposed decoration were foreign to him, he knew the setting—Old Leigh and its surroundings—very intimately from childhood, and so, with a gust of enthusiasm, he summarised his task: 'The problem was to pierce the skin of building which had spread over the hillsides, plant them again with trees, mentally demolish that ugly gasometer and the railway that has cut through the fishing village, and then rebuild the wharves, people them with those oddly dressed Cromwellian figures, fill the estuary with white-sailed ships-of-the-line—and there would be the picture'.

But how was he to begin? It is interesting to recall these early hesitating steps. He resolved that a period of 'learning' must precede any attempt at reconstruction. First then, he borrowed the local history book from the library, to try to gain some idea of the subject's limitations and possibilities. As this was not very helpful, he drew up a questionnaire, characteristic of his methodical approach, and submitted it to the author, an historical scholar and archaeologist of some note: 'Year 1652. 1. Commonwealth Navy frequently anchored off Leigh Road, so one may assume the existence of store-houses, etc? 2. Where or what was Leigh Road? Blake was refitting for two months—sixty men o' war—Penn, Lawson, Dean, reinforced by 1200 soldiers. 3. What was the extent of Leigh at that time? 4. Was there a main road near the shore? 5. Can one assume the new (existing) wharf to be approximately on the site of the old works? 6. Might there have been wharves further west? 7. Would there have been graving docks, etc? 8. Could large ships come in near to the shore? 9. What about Canvey Island and the marshes? Hadleigh Castle? No rectory? Leigh Hall 300 yards east?'

Armed with the answers to these questions, he went down to Old Leigh on a fine spring weekend, to spy out the land and make studies. He was always an artist first, and so the quality of 'seeing' was his major preoccupation: from this would flow ideas and convincing reality. To revisit the neighbourhood and setting of his painting was of fundamental importance. He filled his sketchbook with pencil drawings of old houses which he hoped were typical, trees, the rippling hills. Structural facts were important: how a chimney stack joins the roof, how the branches of a tree really sprout from the main stem.

When the tide came in, he hired an old fisherman to take him out in his boat the *Saucy Ann*, to 'observe the relative tones of sea, shore, and sky'. In his inexperience, he attempted to sketch in oils from the heaving boat, while the old fisherman humorously made movements 'to check the pitching, sir', which seemed rather to add to his difficulties.

His preliminary studies continued in London, with the searching-out of information on Cromwellian shipping, costumes and armour. The Print Room of the Victoria and Albert Museum supplied a box full of fine 17th-century Dutch engravings of dockyard scenes and ships, many of which he confessed later to have surreptitiously traced off! A prominent feature of the painting would show a ship heeled over for repairs, and he found evidence to explain this delicate operation. Many other interesting little facts now came together, and at last the picture began to form in his mind.

His first pen and ink scribble of the design was produced after 'prolonged browsing' over his accumulated material, and contained the seed of all that was to come. A second scribble clarified the shapes without radical change. This looked promising, so he enlarged it, copying now, and squared up the result for transference on to his cartoon, or working drawing.

The cartoon was yet another stage in the 'learning' of the subject. Traditionally, the artist will use it to make all major decisions about size and shape, so as to eliminate such problems from the final surface. In this instance, this penultimate stage fully justified itself, by exposing areas of vagueness in the design, which involved him in further studies. In particular, his ignorance of the functioning of sailing ships as pieces of machinery, with their masses of masts and spars and rigging, led him to make 'numberless drawings' of contemporary ship models at the Science Museum. To complete his understanding, he found it necessary to trace the various ropes 'literally from end to end, from the stanchion to which the one end was secured, to the spar or sail which was moved by its other extremity'. He concluded that 'the effect of truth cannot be obtained without this understanding of cause and effect'.

'Admiral Blake' was completed for exhibition at the Royal Academy in 1933, the actual labour of painting having occupied the previous winter. Sir William Rothenstein praised it for its 'convincing presentation of an event which took place at Southend more than three centuries ago', but also for its 'imaginative vision':

Mr Sorrell's powers of invention, his sense of the dramatic essence of life, give a high value to his work. In everything he does lie power and conviction and he has a poetical vision which makes him as one of the great company of English poets and painters.

With hindsight, 'Admiral Blake' can also be claimed as Alan Sorrell's first serious attempt at 'reconstruction'. All the elements that characterise his later work are already at play in this first unconscious exercise. His ambition was still to be a mural painter, but he was already discovering that his sure strength lay as a draughtsman, and this and necessity impelled him to other possibilities.

The Southend scheme continued to occupy him until about 1936. In the previous year he made the first of many trips abroad, to Iceland, and exhibited the drawings resulting from this journey at Walker's Galleries in New Bond Street on his return. A wild untamed landscape, fantastic rock formations, and strangely twisted trees, always made a strong appeal to his romantic imagination, and Iceland was no exception, though the heavy stylisation of these early drawings disappears from his later work.

It was in 1936, according to his own account, that archaeology as such

Admiral Blake's Fleet Refitting at Leigh:
mural painting at Southend Central
Library, 1933.

Working drawing for reconstruction
of supposed post-Roman church at
Caerwent, 1938.

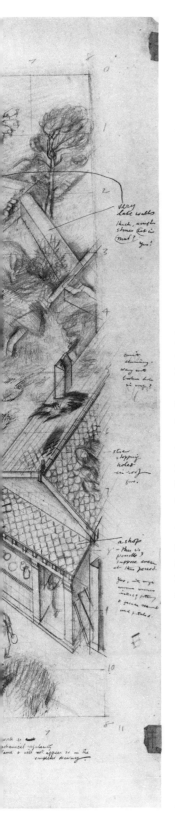

first stirred his interest. He was staying in Leicester by chance while Dr Kathleen Kenyon's excavations of the Roman forum were in progress. This was a busy scene which he recorded in a drawing. The drawing was shown to Sir Bruce Ingram, editor of *The Illustrated London News*, who proposed to publish it alongside a 'restoration' of the forum from the same viewpoint, upon which artist and archaeologist should collaborate.

The drawings duly appeared in February 1937. The immediate result was a request from Dr (later Sir) Mortimer Wheeler for a reconstruction drawing of the Roman assault on the eastern entrance of Maiden Castle, which would incorporate the evidence of his recent and widely publicised excavations: this appeared in *The Illustrated London News* in the following December. Sir Cyril Fox and V. E. Nash-Williams of the National Museum of Wales were also keenly enthusiastic. With them, Alan Sorrell worked in close collaboration between 1937 and 1940 on a series of archaeological reconstructions for the Museum, chiefly of Welsh sites of the Roman occupation, and for the first time, archaeology dominated his artistic output.

Two of these drawings—one of Roman Caerwent, and the other of the legionary fortress at Caerleon—are panoramic views, and others are more intimate scenes, with Roman houses and other structures: all have a high eye-level. The advantages of the high viewpoint had already been explored in the Southend decorations. In these drawings, Alan Sorrell returned to the rigorous preparations that had characterised those early historical-romantic works. The 'learning' of each subject was made easier in this case by the labours of scientific excavation, but in the absence of historical comparisons, the imaginative leap required to bring the past to life was the greater. Roman Britain, in particular, had scarcely been treated by an artist before, and certainly not by one disciplined by reference to specific sites and archaeological fact. To be true to fact, and also imaginatively and artistically true, and therefore convincing, was a considerable task.

In his working methods, he naturally drew upon his experience of mural painting, and favoured a gradual approach. A visit to the chosen site was always his most important source of information—not only to study, with the archaeologist, the visible remains, but also to learn the rise and fall of the ground, and the character of the landscape, trying always to 'get inside the minds of the old builders, and savour something of their problems and achievements'. Then, from maps, plans, photographs and his own sketches would grow the first scribble of the design, which developed—precisely as in the mural paintings—through a series of preliminary sketches, up to a full-size 'cartoon', and thence to the final work. The 'cartoon' was submitted in each case to Fox and Nash-Williams, with points for elucidation written in the margin; they returned it with their answers: it was a working drawing in the fullest sense. He found this gradual approach the most convenient way of handling complex material, and was to use it for the rest of his life, broadened and simplified at last, but fundamentally unchanged.

The War interrupted these activities. He served in the RAF, first in a model-making section, and later at the Air Ministry as a camouflage officer, assisting in the siting, planning and camouflaging of aerodromes.

This latter was an unusual but evidently worthwhile occupation, and involved the spray-painting of acres of runway with patterns of hedge and field and wood, to deceive the enemy bomber, and the surveying of these works from the air. A comparison of his pre- and post-War archaeological work would bring out a decided advance in his control of aerial perspective, which surely owed much to this wartime experience! At every opportunity, he recorded the transient scenes and buildings around him, producing many drawings, several of which were bought by the War Artists' Commission, and went to the Tate and the Imperial War Museum.

He returned to the Royal College of Art in 1946, but his long association with that body ended two years later, in the fracas involving the dismissal of almost the entire teaching staff, following the appointment of a new principal. In 1947 he married the watercolourist Elizabeth Sorrell, and moved back to Essex, where they began a family. He now made the bold decision to live entirely by his work, and resolved to do so by developing the archaeological reconstruction. He renewed his connection with the National Museum of Wales, and *The Illustrated London News*, and was soon busily engaged.

One of the first of these reconstructions was a fine drawing from 1949 of the Roman villa at Llantwit Major. Nash-Williams had written to him in 1938: 'I wish you could see the Roman villa I am opening up. It is in an extraordinary state of preservation and in every way a most interesting site'—but the War had intervened, and excavation and reconstruction were delayed by ten years. Other reconstructions at this time were chiefly of Roman sites. A notable exception was a group of drawings—the first dating from 1949—of the Viking and Prehistoric settlements at Jarlshof in the Shetland Islands, where the archaeologist was John Hamilton.

Alan Sorrell's work was not limited to sites in the British Isles. He contributed three large reconstructions of Knossos, Jericho and Mohenjo-daro to the Festival of Britain in 1951. In 1954 he was sent by *The Illustrated London News* to Greece and Istanbul to gather information for reconstructions at half a dozen sites—among them Mycenae, the Agora at Athens, Nestor's palace at Pylos, and the primitive Greek settlement at Emporio on Chios—and he seized the opportunity to make many drawings.

He worked in England with Professor Ian Richmond on the Carrawburgh Mithraeum on Hadrian's Wall. He was closely involved with the London and Guildhall Museums for many years. In 1954, working with Professor Grimes, he produced drawings of the Walbrook Mithraeum, whose excavation aroused keen public interest.

The Ministry of Works (now the Department of the Environment) was considering ways at this time to popularise the many ancient monuments in its care, by making them more accessible and intelligible to the general public. Travelling exhibitions had already been mounted with some success, using photographs, diagrams and text to explain aspects of the development of the medieval castle and abbey. In 1956, Hadrian's Wall was under consideration for a venture of a similar sort. The material to hand included a number of small models, but for a fuller and more adequate visual treatment, reconstruction drawings were required, and Alan Sorrell was approached to supply them.

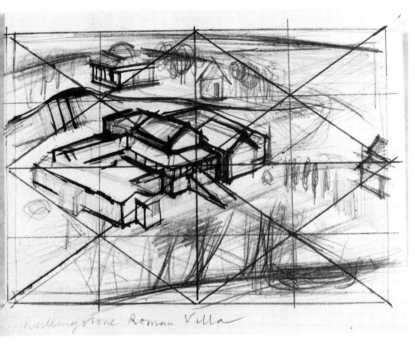

Above left Lullingstone
Roman Villa 1960, first
sketch for reconstruction.
Left Lullingstone Roman
Villa, second sketch.

Above Lullingstone Roman
Villa, 'cartoon' stage, 1961
(see colour plate 3).

In late May, therefore, he travelled up to the Roman Wall, and spent three days visiting the sites. They were: Housesteads Fort, the civil settlement outside the walls of the Fort, and the Roman supply station at Corbridge. Housesteads was visited 'on a characteristically stormy day', and the storm survived into the reconstruction, expressive of wildness and isolation. Returning home to his studio, he set to work with accustomed ease and assurance, and within two days had completed the Corbridge drawing, while the reconstructions of Housesteads occupied no more than four days apiece. A smaller drawing, of Harrow's Scar Mile-castle and Willowford Bridge, also belongs to this period.

Soon after, the drawings were shown to the Minister, Lord Molson, who was excited by their possibilities. He agreed that this talent should be more widely employed by the Ministry, and in fact, a series of reconstructions was commissioned, beginning with drawings of three Edwardian castles in Wales, Conway, Harlech and Beaumaris, produced with the assistance of Dr Arnold Taylor. This led on, in 1957, to further drawings, of Stonehenge, Minster Lovell Hall in Oxfordshire, and the Jewel Tower at Westminster, and to official approval of the scheme in an answer given in the House of Commons: 'The Ministry of Works are anxious to enable the general public to visualise what ancient monuments looked like in the days when they were in use. Mr Alan Sorrell has therefore been employed to carry out drawings . . .'. Thereafter, the scheme broadened rapidly, to embrace most of the more popular sites in the country; each site was to have its drawing, a photograph of which would go on display, for the use of visitors. The reconstructions would not be claimed to be exact, but they would be as accurate as archaeological and historical advice could make them, and they would give the visitor a much clearer idea of the significance of the ruins that lay before him, than had been possible before.

A small but significant change in his working methods was made possible at some of these sites, such as Tintern Abbey, or Kenilworth Castle, or Jedburgh Abbey, where the buildings remain substantial, even in ruin. At such sites, rather than confine his preliminary studies to disjointed pencil sketches, he was able to concentrate his energies in a single careful drawing, using as nearly as possible the viewpoint which he proposed to take in the reconstruction. In this way, quite simply, he used the evidence of his eyes, banishing for a time all thoughts of archaeology from his mind, while he grew absorbed in 'a stealthy consideration of angles' or 'an equally stealthy consideration of two-dimensional patterns', and the projections and recessions of form. There was no better way of assimilating the necessary information. From this study, the reconstruction would later develop in a natural growth.

This work for the Ministry occupied him intensively for four or five years, and intermittently for a longer period. His last twenty years until his death in 1974 were indeed the happiest and most productive of his life. With his archaeological drawings he had opened up a new field for the artist, which he continued to exploit successfully and with distinction. His commissions grew many and varied, with drawings for books, television and museums throughout the country. At the same time, he was able to turn a searching eye on the contemporary world. In 1957, for instance, when he could hardly satisfy the demand for archaeological reconstruc-

Silchester: Christian church 1972: first sketch.

tions, he embarked on a series of drawings recording the building, at Hinkley Point in Somerset, of an atomic power station—a project which continued through five years, stage by stage, from muddy site and sandy shore, to its grand culmination in glass and concrete. Again, in 1962, he travelled in Egypt and Nubia for two months, to 'record' in drawings the ancient temples of the Nile, under threat of destruction by the building of the new High Dam at Aswan. In both cases, he worked with a keen sense of the process of history in the making, and was pleased to assert, here also, the value of an artist's contribution, complementing the exhaustive but nerveless mechanical recording of the camera.

More directly personal were his imaginative paintings, with their evocative titles—'The Facade', 'The Fallen Emperors', 'The Stone Men', 'Agamemnon's Homecoming', 'Via Appia', 'An Ancient Place'. Many of these derived, in his own words, 'from a mysterious or haunting experience'; often, they represent a mature rehandling of themes and thoughts long dormant. 'Via Appia', for instance, drew its inspiration from an experience of his student days in Rome; 'Agamemnon's Homecoming' from drawings made at Mycenae; and 'The Facade', which shows squatters dwelling meanly in a splendid ruin, almost certainly sprang from an observation of his RAF days, of the incongruous juxtaposition of ancient and temporary buildings. A strong characteristic of these paintings is a sense of the decay of a noble past, and this and their treatment, in its starkness and drama, links them inevitably with his

Below Silchester Christian church 'cartoon'.

Bottom Silchester Christian church: additional stage.

archaeological drawings. Once again, one realises how central to his work was the attitude which informed his archaeological reconstructions, and how deeply it was interfused in his imagination almost from the beginning.

Mark Sorrell

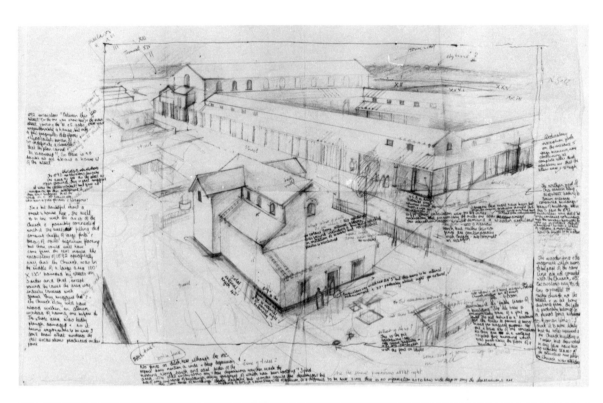

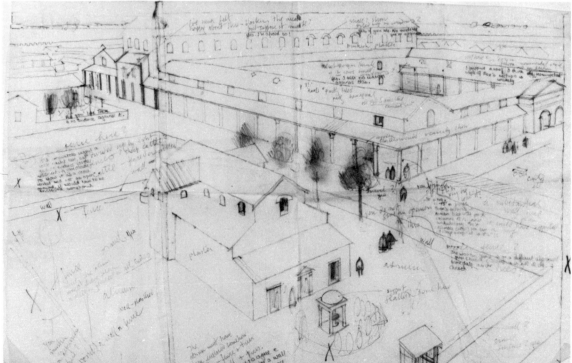

The Artist and Reconstruction

(Reprinted with permission from *Current Archaeology* No 41, Volume IV, No 6. This article is an expansion of a paper originally read at a seminar on the reconstruction of Roman buildings, at the Institute of Archaeology in March 1972.)

I once heard Kenneth Clark describe some paintings and drawings as 'visual records pickled in style'. It is a curious phrase, but was clearly intended to mean that factual recording is only convincing when it is seen through a personality. Obviously, the more potent the personality, the more vivid will be the resulting painting or drawing: we have only to look at a really good work to recognise that. I think this 'pickling in style' can well be applied to drawings which record or reconstruct archaeological subject matter, be it Roman forts, medieval abbeys, or anything else.

As you probably know, I am an artist, and not an archaeologist: this, of course, was never a secret, but I shall feel happier now that I have come clean about it. There are certain advantages in being an outsider. For instance, I do not know too much, and that in itself puts me in a strong position, because I can see the wood without being too keenly aware of the trees.

It is important to remember that European visual art has always been primarily concerned with historical reconstruction, or rather, was so concerned until the advent of the Impressionists in the middle of the nineteenth century, when the artist became enthralled in the pursuit of ephemeral effects of light and colour. Perhaps contemporary art should not be mentioned in the same sentence as 'historical reconstruction'; 'incompatibility' may seem the appropriate word in this context, but it sounds very much like divorce court language, and in fact I fear a divorce may have taken place.

But this is a digression, for I am thinking of traditional European art, of all the reconstructions of the Crucifixion, and of innumerable incidents in Biblical history, from the finding of Moses to Holman Hunt's marvellous and passionately felt 'Scapegoat'. Naturally, there have been many failures: there is a fearful picture called 'Israel in Egypt' by Sir Edwin Poynter, which totally fails as a convincing reconstruction, not because there is anything wrong archaeologically (the artist tied himself into knots to get all the details correct), but because it is so inartistic, a mere conglomeration of unassimilated facts.

Since mankind's preoccupation with destruction rivals his love of construction, there are countless fine reconstructions of battles and sieges, many of them done with such particularisation, that one feels the victorious generals and colonels were breathing down the artists' necks all the time. And they were not just scenes of blood and butchery: there is a famous engraving of the Battle of Naseby (it is reproduced in Trevelyan's *English Social History*). The opposing armies are shown in battle array, rigid troops of cavalry and infantry, with cannon filling the gaps. There they are, face to face, just before the commencement of the action. Trees, hedges and houses are all drawn with as much loving care as the actors in the tragedy. It is a fine work of art, and a valuable 'reconstruction', though, oddly enough, we would never dream of referring to it in that way. In fact, it is a testimony to the indivisibility of art and reconstruction. The only reconstructions which are normally outside the realm of art are those relating to archaeology, and this is unfortunate, because the great quality of a work of art is its intensity of visual expression: obviously, it is a loss to archaeology if reconstructions are enfeebled by the lack of this vital quality, which has brought life to every other facet of human recollection.

I think we have to decide whether archaeology (and, with it, archaeological reconstruction) is linked with what we know as humanistic culture, or is merely a technological offshoot. I, of course, am all for humanistic culture with its imponderables, rather than the precise formulation of factual information which is technology. But it must be stressed here that precision to a hair's breadth is an essential quality in all good art ('good art' is a misnomer, since art is either 'good art' or non-art). But good art is an extension of sensibility, and not a loose and sloppy attitude towards facts. The vital point is that in the final assessment, archaeology deals with humanity—that is, people in their environment of nature and architecture. People have never been able to live without art, and archaeology, which is the study of people and the interpretation of their activities in the past, cannot be properly considered without it.

When we accept this concept of archaeology—that it is the study of people in their environment—then buildings can take their place, literally, in the picture. No longer shall we be expected to tolerate the dumpy little figures which are supposed to 'give scale' to their surroundings: rather must the actors in the comedy or drama be actively engaged, walking along streets, defending fortifications, worshipping in temples, and so on. They will be enveloped in atmosphere, under a moving sky, sheltering from a rainstorm or buffeted by the wind, and the artist will convince us that the ugly little stubs of wall (all too carefully tidied up), which are so often preserved as the final achievement of the archaeologist, are merely indications of what were once upon a time the dwelling places of people very much like ourselves.

Reconstruction drawing has now become respectable. Indeed, it is being declared openly, in the most abandoned way, that Phase One is the excavation, Phase Two is the report, and Phase Three is the reconstruction. This declaration is important, because it means that Phase Three is no longer a more or less casual afterthought with the proviso 'If funds permit' writ large, but is recognised as the logical prolongation and culmination of Phase Two. Ideally, the artist should work with the archaeologist from the very beginning of the project, and it remains the ideal even if it is not always possible in practice. But he should really not try too hard to be one of the team, because, as I said above, it is not good for him to know too much. So long as he is not brought in when it is all over, like an undertaker, to tidy up the corpse and see that the last rites are conducted with due propriety, all will be well. Or rather, all will be well if the artist is recognised as the revivalist who will induce the corpse to behave once again as a living being, and he can do this if the archaeologist will help him.

This help can take many forms. The excavation report is the obvious first choice, though I must admit that I have often been intimidated by the extraordinary profusion of technical terms and a professional jargon which, for me at any rate, becomes a kind of smoke screen, obscuring rather than revealing the subject of the exercise. I suppose the purist would say that a report should be factual only, but as archaeologists do always have opinions, it would certainly make things easier for everybody if the opinion were embodied in the report, even in the form of an appendix. No one likes to commit himself, and I remember on more than one occasion I have been strenuously urged to put some smoke 'to cover up'. Temperamentally, I find this a very difficult proposition—and, anyway, how nice it is to be able to adopt a holier-than-thou attitude!

I would like to make a strong plea for the contouring of site plans. No doubt the shape of the land has altered in the course of centuries, but contouring would at least help to give a general idea of its shape. And then—sections through the site: as many of them as possible, and not just ditch and rampart. The plan, the first essential, is woefully inadequate, especially when slopes and land depressions are involved. Think how limited is the validity of a plan of, say, Harlech Castle: who could imagine the dramatic character of its topography without detailed contouring and sections from sea level to the tops of the towers? Very few reports today include good accurate drawings of architectural remains, though the Victorians often did wonderful work of that kind: there are two great tomes on Fountains Abbey, full of the most meticulous and beautiful drawings, sections and plans, with Turneresque landscape engravings, absolute completeness. I suppose Schools of Architecture are no longer interested in making measured drawings and surveys of such material, but reports could be enormously improved by such additions.

The scale-model is another kind of reconstruction, much favoured by some museums because of its third dimension, which makes it a good centre-piece. But in my opinion (and it is no business of mine to be critical), if the aim is to convince the spectator of the reality of the past, the model fails because it always looks like a model. It fades and gets dusty, bits come unstuck and fall off, the little trees are so clearly pieces of coloured sponge on matchsticks, and, worst of all, there is no endless surrounding landscape, no air or sky—and there always seems to be someone looking through the glass case from the other side. Then there are isometric projections, technical exercises in unreality: they give us glimpses of a never-never land where no man or woman ever walked or breathed.

A most impressive form of archaeological reconstruction is the actual full scale rebuilding of structures and earthworks. A brilliant example of this technique is at The Lunt Roman fort near Coventry, where Brian Hobley brought in the Royal Engineers to erect a timber gateway, fashioned by them in their workshops and assembled by them on the site. It was a remarkable exercise, though, regrettably, the soldiers were not garbed in the Roman fashion and commands (and asides) were not shouted or spoken in the provincial Latin of 100 AD. There, I think, is a point: we cannot achieve the wholeness of complete illusion when there is a bungalow in the background, a girl in a miniskirt in the middle distance, and a corporation official in blue in the foreground. But the last thing I want to do is to carp at this fine achievement, which I believe will prove to be the first of many such physical reconstructions in this country. At the Lunt, not only has the Gateway been reconstructed, but two sections of the turf defensive embankment complete with timber defences and wall-walk have been built, and also a great granary with its supporting timbers set in the old Roman post-holes.

I have said very little about what might be called the mechanics of the job, and before doing so I would like to deal with photography, whose importance to the reconstructor has been much overrated. It is a misfortune that we have become accustomed to what might be called the photographic aspect of appearances. The impact of a massive and ceaseless flood of propaganda has succeeded in conning the majority of us into believing that, not only does the camera tell the truth, but also (and this is even more ludicrous), that human beings really see what the camera registers. It is no good blaming the camera of course, for, being brainless, it clearly has no sensibility, no power of selection, and has only a single mechanical eye to register its two dimensional blots of black and white and grey. Having had our appreciation of visual form almost destroyed by monochrome photography, now colour photography is rapidly mechanising our sense of colour, and a blue sky with scarlet tulips well to the fore on green grass, is held up to us as being pretty good. The bad influence of the camera has led us to accept and very often prefer casual confusion of shape to the ordered clarity which we find in a good drawing.

I say all this because I want to point out that the artist's approach to actuality is far removed from the popular photographic aspect of appearances: it is at the same time more convincing as truth, and far less imitative than the dull registration of unappreciated shapes as recorded by the camera. I don't want to give an impression of bias, so I will readily agree that photography can be useful if a record of the number of bricks in a fragment of wall is required—that is, where only two dimensions need be taken into consideration; and the same kind of value can be seen in air photos where, again, only two dimensions come into the picture. I have had to use photographs in my work, almost always because I have not been allowed sufficient time to make enough drawings, but I have never found them satisfactory, and when I have been foolish enough to be guided by them, I have always discovered that they falsified the true visual facts. Angles in photographs are always wrong and, of course, spatial values are practically non-existent.

I recently made a drawing in the Sheldonian Theatre at Oxford—it was a record of the Encaenia ceremony—and the subtle curved form of the galleries presented a difficult problem of drawing. However, I managed to estimate the shapes in what I felt was a satisfactory way. Then I was given an illustrated guide to help me, and was much disturbed to find that a photograph taken, as it happened, from my own viewpoint, showed the galleries with a much sharper curve, which gave a totally different impression of the scene. But on the next page was a drawing, done in the 18th century, also from the same viewpoint, with flat curves as in my own drawing, and I thought this was a very interesting vindication of the human vision as opposed to the mechanical eye.

If my advice were asked, I would say: 'Never amend a drawing to agree with a photograph: always trust the human eye'. This applies to the use of perspective, too. We are all familiar with the principles of perspective, which have governed European representational art for four hundred years, and which are as fundamental to the working out of an archaeological reconstruction drawing as they were to some Baroque masterpiece—the establishing of a plan in perspective and the fixing of a standard of measurement derive from this study. I sometimes make a grid of squares on a plan and then project it in perspective on my drawing paper. This enables me to relate buildings and streets in a rational way, but mechanical methods of this kind need to be used as warily as the photograph, and must be subject to imaginative correction: once again, it is the human eye that is always right, and not mere mechanical correctness.

The archaeologist can supply the facts, but it is desirable for the artist to walk over the site, plan in hand—and it should be a plan with plenty of space around the built-up area, for so often it is the surrounding landscape and the rise and fall of the land which explain the character of the buildings. It is fascinating to discover that they will disappear from view because of these topographical variations. A high viewpoint has much to commend it, and I like to be able to look down at buildings and into courtyards. On one occasion, it was queried on the grounds that 'the Romans did not have helicopters', and I think I murmured something about 'a cloud of angels', or something like that.

The question of scale is intriguing; convincing reality is a strange and difficult objective to encompass—one would think that the larger the scale the stronger would be the impact of reality. But this is not so, for after a certain point we reject the image, which by its enlargement ceases to have the hypnotic actuality of a dream and becomes, unsuccessfully of course, the competitor of the thing itself. I am sure that if that Victorian horror 'Israel in Egypt' had been smaller in scale (it is ten and a half feet in length), it would have succeeded in hypnotising us into believing it as true. But not only is this picture too large, but in addition it batters us with pedantic detail, so that our imagination has no chance at all to function, and we are left flattened and bored. This is an instance of non-art, whereas the reconstruction which is conceived as a work of art has that super-realism, the realism of the dream, which fixes for ever the image of the scene or incident or personage depicted. One has only to remember paintings by Breughel, Constable or Samuel Palmer to recognise this. No accumulation of detailed accuracy can take its place, but there is no reason on earth why the two qualities should not go together or coalesce.

Roman Britain has occupied a large place in my own work: there is a simplicity about it which is attractive, but a colonial-type dullness too. The Romans sprang no surprises in their planning, and were the most predictable of builders. You can always be reasonably sure of right-angled turns in their structures, while their elevations were never very far from the proportions of the Orders, even in Roman Britain. The skyline must have been dull too, with no chimneys to break the long horizontals—very like those dreadful contemporary housing estates which are now ruining the outskirts of our towns and villages. Such skylines demand clouds above them; perhaps the foamy shapes of cumulus clouds are means by which some sort of artistic unity can be achieved. And drifting smoke, that age-old symbol of habitation, can help, too.

I have not touched on the problem of colour. My own taste inclines to what is called 'limited colour', that is, one does not strive to emulate the vivid green of the grass or the brilliant orange-red of tiles, or the tawny brown of brickwork, for to do so would be to puncture the atmosphere which it is so important to retain. In fact, a good picture does not project beyond the frame, but recedes from it, and is contained within its own world.

I have used the term 'reconstruction drawing' a good many times in this paper, though I do not like it very much. However, sometimes it is convenient to employ it; but it becomes really objectionable, to me, at any rate, when it is used as a caption to a specific drawing. Why should it be used? We never entitle 'The Crucifixion' 'Reconstruction of the Crucifixion', but accept it as the thoughtful opinion of the artist, based on as much literary and historical evidence as was available. And so it should be in archaeology. If an archaeologist is sufficiently confident to (shall we say) *condone* a reconstruction, it surely should be boldly proclaimed as 'So and so in 250 AD', or whatever it might be. If he has a lingering doubt, there could be added an asterisk, and in small print, preferably upside down, the word 'perhaps'. But on second thoughts that does not greatly appeal to me! Even worse than 'reconstruction' is 'Artist's impression', which suggests something fuzzy and completely undependable, or, alternatively, one of those deplorable perspectives of blocks of flats one sometimes sees in *The Times*—only they are not fuzzy, but just hard boiled.

To sum up: a reconstruction drawing—call it what you will—can be the vital final step in an archaeological study. By taking this step we can get inside the minds of the old builders, and savour something of their problems and achievements. The visual apprehension of the artist, disciplined in the most rigorous manner by the facts assembled by the archaeologist, can make a valuable contribution to the search for the truth about the past, which, I suppose, is what archaeology is all about.

I cannot finish this paper without saying how very kind and helpful archaeologists have always been when I have worked with them. I am sure I must often have sorely tried their patience, but never once have I been rebuffed, and looking back, I think this is most extraordinary. I do say 'Thank you' in a truly sincere and wholehearted way—and may we have many more meetings and collaborations!

Ancient Britain

Star Carr
North Yorkshire

The Mesolithic hunting camp at Star Carr in the Vale of Pickering, near Scarborough in Yorkshire, was excavated between 1949–51 by Professor Grahame Clark. The occupation area was found to be small, only 184–201 square metres at most; it was sited on a gravel promontory, artificially extended, on what had once been the northern shore of a shallow lake. Birch brushwood had been thrown down into a reed swamp on the lake's edge, and weighted with stones and lumps of clay to make a rough platform, upon which insubstantial dwellings may have been erected. The site had been periodically abandoned, and was occupied probably only during the winter months and early spring; it was too confined to have supported more than three or four family groups.

A temporary camp of Mesolithic hunters at Star Carr, Yorkshire.

The bones of slaughtered animals were plentifully scattered over the whole area. The remains of some 160 red deer were found, and easily predominated: there were also quantities of bones of wild oxen, elk, roe deer and wild pig, some beaver and other carnivores and rodents, and several water-birds. The jaw bones of the red deer and elks had been broken open to extract the marrow. Curiously, no direct evidence of fishing came to light, though part of a wooden paddle was recovered, and many barbed spearheads, which would seem to indicate that the lake was not neglected. We know from other sites that the Mesolithic people had fishing nets and dug-out canoes.

The principal tools of these huntsmen were of flint and antler, and had been shaped on the site, so that it was possible to study the techniques that had been used. To make spearheads out of antler, narrow splinters had been detached from either the beam or brow tine, by cutting deep parallel grooves, probably with a flint flake, and levering them out with wedges—a most laborious process. The flint implements included axes and adzes for tree felling, microliths for tipping and barbing arrows, scrapers for dressing animal skins, burins and flakes for shaping antler and bone, and awls for drilling holes. These were all unpolished, and the evidence suggests that the tools for heavy work—axes and adzes—must have been re-sharpened many times.

Several other items found during the excavations were less easy to explain. There were, for instance, numerous rolls of birch-bark in relatively good condition. It has been suggested that these were stored as a source of birch resin, which was used for attaching arrowheads to their shafts (in apparent confirmation of this theory, a microlith was found with a lump of resin adhering to it). Alternatively, they could have served as tinder, as also could the many specimens of bracket fungus that were recovered. Their outer skins are said to be especially valuable for this purpose. Lumps of iron pyrites were found nearby, and these, struck against flint, would have provided the necessary spark.

The most exciting find was of twenty or more stag frontlets, severed from the skull, and with the bone pierced in each case in two places, probably for leather thongs to attach to a hood. These may have been worn for stalking deer or for cult purposes, it is uncertain which; but, in the words of the excavator: 'Whether directly functional or whether magical in intent, the masks reflect the overriding preoccupation of the Star Carr people with hunting and in particular with red deer'.

Grime's Graves
Norfolk

Radiocarbon dates of between c. 4300 and 3500 BC have been obtained for material excavated from early Neolithic flint mines in Sussex, some of which appear to have been worked intermittently for an immense span of years. By contrast, mining activity at Grime's Graves in Norfolk belongs to the late Neolithic period, concentrated around 2000 BC, and it lasted for about 200 years. Later occupation of the site, in the Middle Bronze Age, was unconnected with flint extraction.

About 37.5 hectares of a dry Breckland valley were intensively exploited for a high-quality flint (known as 'floorstone'), an almost horizontal band of which runs through the chalk here, varying in depth according to the

Section of flint mine.

slope of the ground. In the north-west of the site, where the land falls away, the floorstone lay within a metre or so of the surface, and could be reached by open-cast mining. The pits in this area were therefore comparatively shallow, and the flint easily extracted, although the soil was not firm enough for galleries to be driven. These shallow pits, it has been suggested, could have been dug in a couple of days, perhaps by farmers visiting the site to collect enough flint for their own needs. On the higher ground, where the floorstone seam lay between 6 and 12 metres down, however, it might have taken several months to sink an adequate shaft to reach it, and this could only be the work of professional miners.

The section shows the characteristic funnel-shape of such a shaft, with

A galleried flint mine at Grime's Graves.

its upper levels battened to prevent loose material falling on to the miners' heads. When the harder chalk was reached, the sides became more nearly vertical, and at floorstone level radiating galleries were dug, to follow the seam for as far as seemed safe and practical, which in one case was for up to 18.3 metres from the base of the shaft. Two inferior bands of flint—'topstone' and 'wallstone'—were dug through to reach the coveted floorstone, and were not exploited unless, for some reason, the floorstone was found to be patchy and poor. This seems to have been the case in Pit No 15 (excavated in 1939 and now roofed over), where the floorstone galleries are very short, and some wallstone has been extracted; and where also, significantly, a chalk mother-goddess and other emblems of fertility were found.

The chief tool used by the miners was the red deer antler, from which all save the brow tine would have been broken, probably by heating. This gives the implement a pick-like appearance, but it is more likely to have been used as a lever, the point being driven into natural fractures in the chalk with a flint hammerstone. Scores of these 'picks' have been found in each of the excavated shafts. Polished flint and stone axes, the long bones of wild oxen, and even, in one of the open-cast pits, a human femur, were also occasionally used.

The extracted flint was drawn to the surface in skin bags or baskets, attached to the end of a rope made of plaited leather. Marks found at the top of Pit No 1 indicate that a beam or tree trunk was probably laid across the pit, to prevent the load dragging on the sides of the shaft. All about the mineheads, flint-knapping 'floors' to a thickness of 1.5 metres have been found, where the extracted material was roughly shaped into axe-heads and other tools. These would then have been peddled through the countryside. The scale and sophistication of the mining operations point to a continuing demand, and suggest a more than local distribution. Excavations have as yet failed to locate the miners' huts, but it is to be presumed that they were somewhere hereabouts.

Avebury
Wiltshire

The primitive significance of the circles at Avebury and Stonehenge is lost and forgotten. Their antecedents cannot be traced with any certainty. No obvious Continental parallels have been found. That they fulfilled a religious function, and were the product of a vigorous and centralised native culture in the centuries around 2000 BC, is more or less all that can be positively said about them.

However, in recent years archaeologists have been able to establish that Avebury and Stonehenge were not an isolated phenomenon in Britain,

Avebury, from the south.

but were related to a fairly specific type of religious monument, concentrated in, but not peculiar to, their region, and known after Stonehenge as 'henge' monuments. These 'henges' appear to have several things in common: usually they are surrounded by a bank, with the ditch on the inside, making the enclosure useless for defence, and with one, two or even four entrances; they are often sited on low ground, near water; they are not specifically burial grounds, though burials may be associated with them; and they also often contain concentric circles of standing stones or wooden posts. Circles of wooden posts of this kind were found in the henges at Durrington Walls and Woodhenge; similar posted circles in the enclosure on Overton Down (which is a mile south of Avebury, and was originally linked to it by the West Kennet Avenue) were later replaced by stones; and there may originally have been timber circles at Avebury itself, since these two sites appear to be contemporary. Stonehenge has peculiarities all its own.

The Avebury enclosure impresses by its immense size: in places it is up to 430 metres across. The ditch was flat-bottomed, about 9 metres deep and 21 metres wide. The spoil from the ditch had been thrown up into an outer bank that must have stood about 5.5 metres high, and been of startling whiteness. This was set back 4.5 metres from the lip of the ditch for most of the circumference, except on the west, where there was apparently no berm, and where the bank was contained by a revetment of chalk blocks. This, and irregularities in the ditch bottom, point to the work having been performed by a number of separate gangs of workmen.

On the inner edge of the ditch stood a great circle of about 100 natural blocks of sarsen. Two smaller circles were placed within this. The Central Circle was about 97.5 metres across, and composed of about 30 stones, with three huge blocks standing in the middle, which are known as The Cove. The South Circle contained about 28 stones, and had a strangely arranged inner group. The so-called Ring Stone stood alone between the South Circle and the southern entrance, but was destroyed in the 18th century. The West Kennet Avenue approaches the southern entrance, where it makes a sharp and awkward turn to the right. Another stone avenue may have led away from the western entrance.

Stonehenge
Wiltshire

Stonehenge as it stands today, the most celebrated and remarkable prehistoric monument in western Europe, is the culmination of a series of building periods. It was not, as Geoffrey of Monmouth would have us believe, shipped out of Ireland by the conjuror Merlin, and re-erected complete on Salisbury Plain. Centuries of patient effort, extraordinary labour and extraordinary skill, were expended on the successive monuments that have stood upon the site.

Phase I at Stonehenge has been dated to about 2600 BC. The beginnings here were modest, almost slight. The total area, enclosed by a roughly cut ditch, had a diameter of about 107 metres. The ditch itself was about 6 metres wide, and varied in depth from 1.3 to 2.1 metres at the maximum. There was a low outer bank, but, unlike at Avebury, most of the ditch material here had been thrown up on the inside: this inner

Stonehenge, phase I,
from the east.

bank must have been about 6 metres wide, and over 1.8 metres high. Immediately inside this, 56 pits had been dug in a lesser circle at an average of 4.9 metres apart. These are the so-called Aubrey Holes, named after their discoverer, the antiquary John Aubrey. Excavations have established that the pits contained neither posts nor stones and, though later cremated burials were found in some of them and in the ditch, their original purpose is obscure. The single entrance was on the north-east: two stones, probably of sarsen, stood in the gap. About 24.5 metres beyond the entrance, a line of four post-holes were found, which have been reconstructed here as a timber triple gateway. Close by, the Heel Stone, a rough block of natural sarsen, was placed, standing about 4.9 metres high. This is the only unshaped sarsen stone on the site. The ditch, banks, Aubrey Holes and 'gateway' were all laid out from a common centre.

The second phase at Stonehenge followed after about 500 years, when the site assumed a position of new importance. The 'gateway' and the two sarsen blocks in the entrance were probably now removed (the stones were replaced in the third phase), and an avenue 12 metres wide, bounded by low banks and ditches, and incorporating the Heel Stone, was built approaching the entrance. This avenue was carefully aligned from the centre of the circle, to extend towards the sunrise at the summer solstice: it led off in a straight length for about 400 metres to the north-east downhill, then curved away east and south-east, ending on the banks of the River Avon. Up this processional way the eighty or so great blocks of bluestone must have been dragged that were set up in a double circle in the centre of the enclosure. They had been floated up the river from the coast, it is thought, after a hazardous journey from the Prescelly Mountains in South Wales, the prime source of this rock. The centre of this bluestone double circle and of all subsequent circles, was about one metre south-south-west of the centre of the earthworks of the first phase.

For some reason, these works were not completed: the unfinished circles of bluestones were dismantled and laid to one side. In the third main

building phase more than 80 huge blocks of sarsen, weighing on average 26 tonnes each, were dragged to the site in the same manner, but this time probably from the Marlborough Downs, about 30 kilometres away to the north. These were set up in the circle and horseshoe that can be seen today. The technical difficulties of moving, siting, shaping and raising such huge stones are astonishing to contemplate. The refinements to which such apparently intractable material was subjected are no less remarkable: the lintels are curved on their inner and outer faces to make segments of an almost perfect circle carpentered together with tongue-and-groove joints, and held in place on the uprights with tenon and mortice. All this was achieved with the most primitive tools, chiefly, it is believed, by pounding the surface with heavy stone mauls, and smoothing it with sarsen grinders.

When the sarsen stones had been set up, about 20 of the bluestones were re-erected in an arrangement within the sarsen horseshoe, and the remainder were probably meant to be placed in the Y and Z holes so-called, which can be seen in the drawing encircling the monument. (The irregular siting of these holes has been attributed to the difficulty of obtaining accurate measurements from the centre with the larger stones in the way.) However, once again, for some reason, the work was never done, and the final arrangement of the bluestones repeats that of the sarsens—a circle within the sarsen circle, and a horseshoe within the trilithon horseshoe.

By c. 1500–1400 BC these works were at an end. To Geoffrey of Monmouth, twenty-five centuries later, it seemed a work of magic: and it is easy to imagine how its powerful symmetry must have awed and swayed the mind of prehistoric man.

Staple Howe
North Yorkshire

This steep-sided chalk knoll rises above 22 metres on the northern edge of the Yorkshire Wolds, overlooking the Vale of Pickering. Excavations organised by Mr T. C. M. Brewster have uncovered two main phases of occupation. In the first, the hilltop was fenced to provide an enclosure for a single oval hut, 9.1 metres by 6.1 metres, with its floor sunk below ground level, and walls of chalk slabs. Remains of an oven were found; there was a hearth near the western end, and the hut entrance was opposite this, with no porch protection.

Later, the area of the enclosure was extended to include the whole of the flat top and upper slopes of the knoll. A stouter palisade was erected: the closely set uprights were tied in to a row of short posts set further back, which were concealed under a platform of earth and rubbish. The one entrance was on the south side, and probably closed by a moveable hurdle.

The single oval hut appears to have been abandoned at about this time, to be replaced by the two round huts shown in the drawing, one at either end of the enclosure. These had porch entrances, opening to the south-east. The hut to the west, which was better preserved, contained features presumably common to both. It was 9.5 metres in diameter, with post holes for timbers to support the roof. An open hearth, the remains of a clay oven, and slots which are thought to have held an upright loom

Stonehenge, at its fullest
development, about
1400 BC, viewed from
the east.

35

Iron Age settlement at
Staple Howe, viewed
from the south-east.

were also found. The roofs are shown weighted down against the wind.

The structure in the centre of the drawing would have been about 2.7 metres square, and was very strongly built, with five post holes, all more than 0.6 metre deep. This has been interpreted as a raised granary; carbonised wheat was found elsewhere on the site.

Much pottery was also found, along with weaving and netting equipment, implements of bone and stone, ornaments of jet, a little iron, and three bronze razors, which have been dated to about 500 BC. Radio-carbon tests on some of the charred grain have produced a date of c. 530 BC. Occupation is unlikely, on structural grounds, to have lasted more than a few decades, and would appear to have ceased by the middle of the 5th century BC.

Heathrow
Middlesex

Practically the whole of this early Iron Age settlement was uncovered in 1944 in a rescue excavation conducted by Professor Grimes, prior to the building of Heathrow Airport.

William Stukeley, the 18th-century antiquary, first discovered the site and called it 'Caesar's Camp', not unreasonably. An engraving in his *Itinerarium Curiosum* shows a rectangular enclosure, lying in the wilderness of Hounslow Heath, with a clearly defined bank and ditch and opposite entrances on north and south sides. When the Heath was enclosed and cultivated, these striking features were almost entirely ploughed away. But the excavation confirmed Stukeley's observations: the ditch, sectioned in one place, was 6.1 metres wide and 2.4 metres deep, and the bank about 3.1 metres high, no doubt originally with a palisade on top.

In the excavation, eleven round huts were found, concentrated in the northern half of the enclosure. The area to the south contained occupation material but no evidence of buildings, and was probably used for folding herds and flocks. The huts were ringed by drainage gullies, at their widest 10.1 metres across. Post holes for roof supports were present in some cases, and more or less absent in others, indicating that the lower walls of some of the huts were probably of turf. Internal features were very slight: some early Iron Age pottery and one cylindrical loom-weight of baked clay were found, and there were one or two hearths; but the hearths were generally outside the huts, where they showed up as burnt oval areas, about a metre across.

Dominating the enclosure was a far more substantial and exciting structure. As excavated, this consisted of two main elements: an inner

The Iron Age settlement at Heathrow, seen from the south-east.

rectangular, flat-bottomed trench, measuring 5.5 metres by 4.57 metres externally, with massive post holes at each of its four corners, and two more flanking the doorway on its eastern side; and an outer rectangle of spaced post holes, measuring overall about 11 metres by 9.5 metres, with the entrance again on the east side, and a possible porch extension shading it. This arrangement immediately suggested a prehistoric temple, aligned east-west, with a solid inner shrine (walled in with timbers laid horizontally) and an outer, open-sided ambulatory or covered walk. The resemblance to the form of the classical Greek temple was remarkable, and here also, it was suggested, was a possible forerunner to the later Romano-Celtic temple form, a number of examples of which have been excavated in Britain. What god or goddess was worshipped here, and whether an altar or images were placed within the shrine, these things are not known, but the timbers of the colonnade had been frequently renewed, suggesting long-term use. There are indications that the site was cleared and marked out for the erection of a true Romano-Celtic temple during the Roman period, after the earlier temple had decayed; but this later work on the sacred site was never carried through to completion.

Maiden Castle
Dorset

The multiple defences of Maiden Castle enclose about 18 hectares of a broad, saddle-backed hill.

The site had a complex history, as Sir Mortimer Wheeler's famous excavations of 1934–37 revealed. The earliest known inhabitants, in Neolithic times, constructed a causewayed camp around the eastern end of the hill; to be overlaid, at no long time after its abandonment, by a Neolithic bank-barrow of extraordinary length, extending west along the hill ridge for about 600 metres. This in turn was deliberately reduced by the hill's later inhabitants, though the line of its parallel ditches must have long remained visible.

These developments took place before 3000 BC. During the Bronze Age the hilltop was apparently uninhabited, and lay so for over two thousand years. Then, in about 350 BC, Iron Age colonists arrived, and proceeded to fortify with a single rampart and ditch the same area at the eastern end as had been previously enclosed in Neolithic times. The small hill fort thus created, with an area of 4–6 hectares, had entrances to east and west, that on the east having a double gateway.

About a hundred years after this the western rampart and ditch and gateway of the small fort were levelled (although their approximate line can still be seen in the drawing, and indeed on the ground), and a new ditch and rampart were thrown out to include for the first time the whole of the present area of the fort. A double gateway was inserted in the new western end, and at about the same time both east and west entrances were equipped with an outer pincer-like hornwork.

Further elaboration of the entrances took place in about 150 BC. The gateways themselves were flanked with high drystone walls, for which large limestone blocks from a quarry 3 kilometres away were used. Two extra ramparts and ditches were added to the southern defences of the town, and a further single line to the north, and the main bank was almost doubled in height; and so the site began to assume its familiar

Maiden Castle from the west, at its fullest development.

form. These changes are attributed to the introduction of the sling into what must have been fierce inter-tribal warfare: fortification in depth put the hostile slingers out of range.

Contact with Belgic settlers from Gaul brought superior pottery and coinage into the settlement in the last few decades before the Roman invasion. The defences were further strengthened and improved, most noticeably by the provision of a rampart walk on the main bank, fenced on its inner side. The streets were remetalled, and the hundreds of insanitary grain storage pits were filled in, presumably to be replaced by barns and sheds.

The end of the settlement with the storming of the more approachable eastern gate by Vespasian and the IInd Augusta Legion in the Claudian conquest, is well known. It is not too difficult to visualise the scene: the dreadful demoralising effect upon the defenders of Roman ballista fire (transforming an almost impregnable stronghold into a hopeless trap), and their inability to reply; the firing of the exterior huts; the Roman advance under cover of the smoke; the taking of the place; the massacre that followed; the subsequent systematic destruction of gateways and defences; the soldiers marching away; the hurried, pitiful burials of the British war dead. The Romans built a new township for the tribesmen down in the valley, at Durnovaria (Dorchester) 3 kilometres away, and here, ultimately, the hilltop population was moved.

Roman Britain

The Lunt Roman Fort, Baginton
Warwickshire

The Lunt Roman Fort from the north-east.

The first Roman fort at The Lunt was apparently constructed at great speed around AD 60, at the time of the Boudiccan rebellion; the excavators were unable to establish its exact size, but it was certainly very extensive. It is possible that the crucial battle in which Boudicca was defeated took place in this area, which would account for the presence of large numbers of troops. The foundation traces in the foreground of the panoramic drawing belong to buildings of this period.

As soon as the danger had past, the bulk of the troops moved on, and the fort was reduced to an area of 1.8 hectares. The main period of its occupa-

tion now commenced, and lasted until about AD 80. By that time, the
greater part of the territory of the Brigantes to the north had been an-
nexed, the Roman conquest of Wales was complete, and Agricola was
already advancing into Scotland. As the military moved up to new
frontiers, the fort was first drastically cut down in area and, very shortly
after, was entirely abandoned and then demolished. There was a brief
spasm of refortification on the site in the 3rd century, but effectively the
life of the fort was at an end.

The drawings relate to the main period of occupation. The gates,
palisades and all buildings were of timber throughout. In this they were
not untypical of Roman military sites of the same date, but in other ways
the fort is unique. Most striking, for the distinctly un-Roman wobble it
created in the eastern rampart, is the intrusive circular feature. This was
about 32.5 metres across, with an entrance 3.1 metres wide on the west
side, and a funnel-like approach. The excavator, Mr Brian Hobley, has
interpreted this unusual arrangement as a *gyrus* or arena, where horses
were broken in, trained and exercised. The discovery is unparalleled in
Britain, although examples are known from elsewhere in the Empire. It
may be significant that the long block on the north side of the *gyrus*
entrance, was a lightly roofed structure, for this may well have provided
stabling for horses. Two shorter buildings east of this block, between
it and the rampart, and the longer pair of buildings west of it, were almost
certainly cavalry barracks. In the panoramic drawing, three plumes of
smoke rise from three ovens against the rampart. The oblique structure to
their right was a granary. The long thatched building beyond may well

The Granary beside the principia.

have been used for storing fodder, and as a tack room. Another granary lay some 15 metres further west, and the whole western corner of the fort was taken up with the *fabrica*, the unit's workshops, whence more plumes of smoke arise.

The courtyard building in the centre of the fort was the *principia*, or headquarters building, occupying its normal position at the junction of the *via praetoria*, from the south gate, and the *via principalis*, connecting east and west gates. Another granary stood to the west of the *principia* (this is shown in the separate drawing). This was 21.3 metres long by 9.1 metres wide, with loading bays at each end, and was raised on 105 wooden pillars, at 1.5-metre intervals. It was roofed with wooden shingles.

The function of a little group of buildings east of the *principia*, adjoining the *gyrus*, is obscure: the excavators found a number of huge water tanks here, and suggest that it may have been an ablution block, where the men washed after their exertions in the *gyrus*. This certainly does not conform to the arrangements of an orthodox Roman bath suite, which, in any case, would not normally be found within the fort, because of the risk of fire.

There were more cavalry barracks in the south-west corner of the enclosure. The whole south-eastern quadrant (shown in the panoramic drawing in course of construction) consisted of one large building, which it was difficult to interpret. It would seem to have been the commanding officer's house, the *praetorium*, but, if so, was of exceptional size, and would prove him to have been a man of considerable importance. The presence of such a large building, and by implication of such a high-ranking officer, suggests that the Lunt was functioning to train not only horses,

but also men; that it was, in fact, a Roman cavalry training school, the first recorded example of such.

The excavations lasted from 1965 to 1973, and during this time a number of the Roman buildings, notably the granary, were physically reconstructed on the site. The Royal Engineers, appropriately, provided the labour, and the wood used was elm, from trees affected by Dutch Elm disease. (Fragments of worked elm and oak were recovered from a water-logged Roman well on the site.) Thus two kinds of reconstruction are available, and may be compared.

Hadrian's Wall Hadrian's Wall consists of four elements: a ditch on the northern side, about 8.2 metres wide, with an average depth of 2.7 metres; the Wall itself, with its turrets, milecastles and forts; a second ditch, the Vallum,

Hadrian's Wall looking
west, near Chesters.

south of the Wall, flat-bottomed, 6.2 metres wide and 3.1 metres deep, with continuous earth banks set back 9.1 metres on either side; and south of the Vallum, a slightly later addition, the Military Way.

The drawing of the Wall near Chesters shows milecastle No 26 in the foreground; two turrets and a further milecastle lie beyond it, after which the land falls steeply to the valley of the North Tyne, where Chesters cavalry fort was situated (not visible).

Hadrian's Wall was 80 Roman miles long, stretching from coast to coast, from Bowness-on-Solway to Wallsend on the Tyne, and it marked the northern frontier of the Roman province after the abandonment of Scotland in the 1st century AD. It was built between AD 122 and 130— begun in the very year of the Emperor Hadrian's visit to Britain. It was to be manned by auxiliary troops, to form the forward line of a military zone that reached back to the legionary fortresses at Chester and York. Restless Brigantia to the south was thick with Roman garrisons and the Vallum was dug to discourage the unfriendly attentions of tribesmen from this side. The efficiency of the Wall was increased by a line of milefortlets and watchtowers which extended for over 40 Roman miles down the Cumberland coast.

The Wall itself was 4.5–4.7 metres high to the wall walk, with a parapet rising about 1.8 metres above that. It ran for long stretches along the ridges of the hills, where steep falls on the north side made the northern ditch unnecessary. At regular intervals of one Roman mile (1481.3 metres), a milecastle was attached to the inner side, with barracks to accommodate 25 to 50 men. Each milecastle was provided with a gateway or sally port through the Wall, wide enough to take wheeled traffic, and through which detachments could issue forth to take the offensive in times of danger. The turrets, placed at intervals of one third of a Roman mile (493.8 metres), were not provided with either a gate through the Wall or a causeway over the northern ditch, and were obviously intended for more static defence. They would have housed soldiers patrolling the wall walk, and signallers who, by an elaborate system, ensured that all these defensive posts were in contact with each other.

In the drawing of Walltown Crags, milecastle No 45 is in the middle distance, with turret No 45A nearer at hand. Beyond, the Wall can be seen 'wonderfully rising and falling'. The Vallum is on the extreme right, lying some distance back from the Wall.

Willowford Bridge lies about 6.5 kilometres west of Walltown. Here the River Irthing flows south-westward through a steep-sided valley with many convolutions on its journey to the sea. The Romans, with their usual directness, made no attempt to skirt round the topographical difficulties caused by this meandering stream, but from a relatively low-lying meadow drove across the river, supporting the Wall on flat arches (defended by turrets at either end), then up the steep bank. Here, as at Walltown, the Wall was stepped on the ascent. A milecastle (No 49) guarded the top of the bank. The fort of Birdoswald lay 0.8 kilometre to the west.

Hardly had the Wall been completed, than there was a fresh, large-scale advance into and re-occupation of southern Scotland, and the Antonine turf wall was built between the Forth and Clyde to mark the new frontier. In the absence of its garrisons, Hadrian's Wall was exten-

Top Hadrian's Wall at Walltown Crags, looking east, as it might have appeared in the 2nd century AD.

sively damaged in raids in AD 197 and again in 296. The third and last great raid occurred in AD 367, when Picts, Scots and Saxons combined and fell upon Roman Britain. Rebuilt in AD 369, the Wall was finally abandoned less than 20 years later, but it is interesting to reflect that, even so, the successful invaders of England came, not over its ruins, but from the south.

Hadrian's Wall
Housesteads
Roman Fort
Northumberland

Housesteads was one of 17 auxiliary forts that were ultimately placed on or near the line of the Wall, at intervals of 6.5–8 kilometres. These were not a part of the original scheme—which had the bulk of the troops stationed on the Stanegate supply road about a kilometre or two to the south—but were added while the Wall building was in progress. The discrepancy in size between the original turrets and milecastles and these forts, capable of housing up to 1,000 men, reflects the changed function of the Wall as the planners were forced to conceive it, from a mere police and customs barrier to a military defensive line in a very real sense.

Housesteads guards the passage through the ridge, at this point, of the Knag Burn, which flows south in a narrow valley. The eastern end of the fort projects several metres east of the great Wall, which descends into the valley from a tower displaced from the fort's north-east angle. The hard basalt on which it was founded must have put the builders to much labour to level the site; it certainly dissuaded them from digging wells. Large tanks were associated with some of the towers, however, probably to collect rain water from the flat roofs, and these tanks may have been supplemented by a piped supply from the Knag Burn. Only two short lengths of protective ditch were dug, on the northern halves of the east and west sides of the fort. The walls were 3.6 to 4.3 metres high, with angle and interval towers (some of them added at a later date), and with

Opposite below Hadrian's Wall: Harrow's Scar Milecastle and Willowford Bridge, looking east.

Housesteads Roman fort, from the south.

an internal earth embankment which carried a secondary wall walk.

The east gate was the main entrance to the fort. From this the *via praetoria* led directly to the *principia* with its arcaded courtyard. The planning was deliberate: that soldiers marching in through the main gate should always see before them, through the gate into the *principia* courtyard, the altars of the chapel in the central room on its opposite side, where the unit's standards would have been kept and displayed. The other rooms contained the offices of the adjutant and of the standard-bearers, whose duties included the administration of the garrison's savings-bank. Here also the commanding officer took his seat on ceremonial or official occasions.

There were six long buildings in the eastern third of the fort, and six more in the western third. Ten of these were barracks, each accommodating 100 men. The additional building in each case was probably used for stabling or as a storehouse.

To the west of the *principia* stood the military hospital. To the south was the commandant's house, built around a courtyard, with a private bath suite to one side. To the north were granaries, and a long building behind them which may have contained workshops. The north-west angle tower was used as a cookhouse, and here a large oven was found. Latrines stood close to the south-east angle: the main sewer passed under the angle and resurfaced about 91 metres down the slope.

The identity of the earliest troops on garrison duty at Housesteads is not known. In the 3rd century, it was the first cohort of Tungrians, an infantry battalion first raised in the Tongres district of Belgium. Later, Frisian auxiliaries may have been quartered here.

Hadrian's Wall
Housesteads
Civil Settlement
Northumberland

From the south gate of the fort at Housesteads, a road led by a causeway over the Vallum to the Roman supply base at Corbridge; and another, branching to the south-west, to the fort at Chesterholm (Vindolanda). The Military Way met them where it skirted the south wall of the fort. Here civil buildings sprang up in the 3rd and 4th centuries. The Vallum by this date had gone out of use, and with it, apparently, had gone the need for a clear line of fire from the fort's defences, for buildings eventually straggled up to and even sheltered under the great Wall itself. No civilian defences were provided, as they were on the Antonine Wall; nevertheless, soldiers' families, traders, time-expired veterans, potters, cobblers and other skilled craftsmen made their homes here, with every appearance of security. Taverns and gambling houses catered for the soldiers in their off-duty hours, but evidence has also been found of at least seven temples, including a Mithraeum, lying beyond the closely packed houses, and there must have been numerous smaller shrines. Most surprising of all, a gateway was opened through the Wall in the 4th century, in the valley of the Knag Burn, to provide for trading with the free peoples in the unenclosed land to the north.

The eastern portal of the south gate of the fort was blocked in about AD 300, during reconstruction of the Wall after the great raid of AD 296 (blocking also occurred in the other gates of the fort, probably with the feeling that so many grandiose entrances had become superfluous). The

The south gate of the fort at Housesteads and part of the civil settlement, as it might have appeared in the 4th century AD.

houses on the main street of the civil settlement (shown in the drawing) must have been rebuilt at about the same time, because both they and the road were aligned with the open west portal. These houses were of the usual narrow rectangular shape, end-on to the street, often terminating in open-fronted shops. The lower storeys were constructed of the local stone, and the upper probably timber-framed, very like surviving medieval dwellings.

The busy and sometimes rather squalid life in the Housesteads civil settlement lasted until the third great raid on the Wall in AD 367, when all external buildings were destroyed and not rebuilt. Thereafter, the women and children moved into the fort along with the garrison, and their presence overcame all old-fashioned military scruples: in the last dark days, the *principia* at last ceased to function as such, and was converted into mess rooms and living quarters, while in the adjutant's office a smith had set up his workshop, and was probably busily turning out arrowheads when the fort was overwhelmed.

Corbridge Roman Station
Northumberland

Corstopitum was the Roman name of this important supply base, sited on the north bank of the River Tyne, 5 kilometres south of Hadrian's Wall. Here, Dere Street, the main trunk road to the north, crossed the east-west road serving the Wall, the Stanegate, and its position at this junction ensured that Corstopitum played a significant part in the history of the northern frontier.

Agricola placed a timber fort, recently discovered, 1.2 kilometres west of here on low ground, on his advance into Scotland in AD 79. After the Scottish conquests had been given up, c. AD 87, and the Stanegate became the front line, the Agricolan fort was moved to its present site to command the Dere Street bridgehead. In AD 122 Hadrian's Wall was built, superseding the Stanegate line, and Corstopitum was evacuated to lie derelict for 15 years. Seventeen years later, with the advance to the Forth-Clyde, Corstopitum again became important as an invasion base: it was reoccupied as a fort and rebuilt in stone. It was overthrown by northern invaders, AD 197, and afterwards rebuilt by Septimius Severus on the grand scale, when it became the supply base for another northern campaign. Had Severus lived longer, Corstopitum might well have been developed into a legionary fortress—there are hints of that intention in the

Corbridge Roman Station: the centre of the supply base from the south-east, as it might have appeared in the 3rd century AD.

layout of the buildings. But again the pendulum swung back from the north, and the frontier was finally fixed on Hadrian's Wall in AD 211. After this, Corstopitum lost its predominantly military complexion and developed into a prosperous town and trading centre of some 14–16 hectares, though it retained close connections with the army. This post-Severan period is shown in the drawing.

The Stanegate is the main road here—Dere Street, about 90 metres to the west, lies out of the top of the picture. Only the central portion of the 3rd-century layout is shown. The long range of buildings on the right is the only part of the grandiose administrative headquarters (planned by Severus to enclose the four sides of a great courtyard 50.3 by 45.7 metres) that was completed at his death. This massive fragment was later probably divided into shops. It overlay, in part, the *principia* and commandant's house of the earlier fort.

Beyond it on the Stanegate was an elaborate fountain, ornamented with statues on pedestals, the water discharging into a cistern and thence into an oblong tank. Beyond this stood a pair of externally buttressed granaries.

The two irregular fortified enclosures on the left side of the street were occupied by legionary craftsmen, armourers and the like, installed here after the idea of creating a legionary fortress had been given up. They supplied the garrison on the Wall with equipment and stores. The irregularity of the walls was due to a bewildering collection of small temples of earlier date by the roadside, which could not be encroached upon.

The gateways of these two enclosures faced each other, and at the end of a short road in each case stood the headquarters building of the compound, the nearer one having a central chapel with a rearward apse, supported on either side by offices for clerks. The small square courtyard buildings inside the nearer compound were officers' houses; the rest were either soldiers' quarters or workshops, with the exception of two buildings in the foreground, both with apsidal ends, which were probably *scholae*— club rooms and shrines combined, for the use of NCOs and men when not on duty. The identical pairs of buildings in the further compound were armourers' workshops.

Reconstructed by Constantius, c. AD 300, and again by Theodosius in AD 369, when a wall may have been put about the town, Corstopitum sinks at length into the obscurity of the Dark Ages. Anglian invaders came, and founded nearby Corbridge, and ruined Roman Corstopitum then became a quarry for building stone for churches, farms and houses over a wide area.

Segontium Roman Fort
Gwynedd

To the west of the great legionary fortresses of Chester and Caerleon, much of Wales was permanently garrisoned throughout the Roman period. Segontium (in the suburbs of modern Caernarvon) was one link in a chain of auxiliary forts that extended around the Welsh coast, perhaps initially to serve as invasion bases, but later to support additional forts that were planted in the interior. Twelve hundred years later, the Edwardian castle at Caernarvon was sited in close proximity to the ruins of this fort: and though that fact alone cannot be taken to prove the

Segontium Roman Fort from the south, as it might have appeared in the 3rd century AD.

dominance of Segontium in the Roman chain, the parallels between the two systems of conquest and occupation are interestingly suggestive.

Segontium was probably founded in AD 78 after the defeat of the Ordovices at the hands of Roman troops, but the earliest reconstruction of the fort in stone is dated to the middle of the 2nd century. It is thought to have been sacked by Welsh tribesmen in AD 197, when Clodius Albinus, the then governor of Britain, withdrew his troops, to make an unsuccessful bid for imperial power. There was certainly extensive rebuilding early in the 3rd century, when the First Cohort of Sunici, auxiliaries recruited in the Rhine-Meuse area, were the garrison. Another period of destruction possibly followed early in the 4th century, and more rebuilding, before the fort was finally abandoned, c. AD 383.

The internal arrangement of buildings followed the familiar pattern of Roman forts and marching camps. The ramparts measured 167.6 by 143.3 metres, enclosing an area of about 1.8 hectares, with four gateways, and a double ditch. In the centre was a headquarters building of orthodox type, with courtyard and basilica. To its right in the drawing is a pair of granaries; to its left the commandant's house, with the open yard of the *fabrica* (workshops) adjoining. All buildings in the rear third of the fort were barracks (except the one shown in the drawing with external buttresses, which was a granary or perhaps a forage store). The remainder of the barracks occupied the front third, and were aligned with the long axis of the fort: they were sub-divided internally, and the cross walls are expressed in the stepped roofs. The two short-axis buildings on the near side may have been stable blocks. A bath house has been inserted near the southern angle. The main bath house stood outside the fort, beyond the ditch.

Traces of a civil settlement have been found on all but the furthest side of the fort. A Mithraeum was uncovered in 1959 in the group of civil buildings on the right. Below the foreground, the land dropped down to the River Seiont, where there was a Roman port. In the distance, across the Menai Straits, lies Anglesey, the scene of fierce early resistance to Roman rule, with the Irish Sea beyond.

London
The Roman City

Londinium is the Latinised form of the Celtic Londinos, a hypothetical personal name, formed from Londos, meaning 'fierce'; but archaeological opinion is against the assumption of a Celtic foundation, since the pre-Roman remains along the river banks are, so far, meagre and scattered. The Roman origins of the city are thought to have been purely military. The decisive factor was the building of the first bridge across the river by the army of Claudius in AD 43, which had as its objective an advance to Camulodunum (Colchester), the native capital of the Catuvellauni, where the Roman capital was also to be established. Direct evidence of a military camp belonging to this early period was found during excavations near Aldgate in 1972.

However, Londinium was never a fortress, and the potential of the site, the river and the bridge was only to be realised by energetic traders following in the wake of the army, who began to settle in the area north of the bridge, along streets that the army may have laid down for them. In the seventeen years following the conquest, their community grew into what Tacitus describes as 'a place not indeed distinguished by the title of *colonia*, but crowded with traders and a great centre of commerce'. Theirs was the town, undefended and sprawling, that Boudicca sacked with horrible slaughter and devastation in AD 60. The marks of this disaster remain to this day, in a layer of burnt red ash containing fragments of Samian ware, coins of Claudius fused by fire, wattle and daub mingled with wall plaster, all found at a depth of between 3 and 4 metres, just above natural ground level, in the area between Gracechurch Street and Walbrook.

The city seems to have recovered rapidly, and in the rebuilding to have been extended far beyond its previous limits, until it comprised much of the area contained within the later walls. Two low hillocks, or knolls, not more than 15.2 metres above river level, marked the eastern and western limits of the site. Leadenhall Market now covers the eastern hill, where the forum and a concentration of the better-class, stone-built houses stood in

Roman times; and St Paul's Cathedral surmounts the western hill.
Further to the east were two small hillocks where now stand the Tower of
London and the Mint, the latter outside the city proper. The site was
bisected by the north-south axial line of the Walbrook, a marshy stream
with a flood-plain up to 91.4 metres in width. The Fleet river bounded
the city on the west.

It is indicative of the growing importance of Londinium that the Procurator—an official directly responsible to the Emperor for all matters
connected with finance and the collection of taxes in the province—seems
to have been based in the city after the Boudiccan rebellion. Also in the

late 1st century great public buildings were constructed, including the forum and basilica, and the Governor's palace. The fort, on the north-west extremity of the city, would have housed the Governor's guards and staff, and was probably built in the early 2nd century. However, the popular idea of a city of classical times, with colonnaded temples and public buildings occurring at regular intervals, did not, of course, obtain here, or indeed anywhere else. Londinium, while it had some regularity in its street plan, must also have had the familiar mixture of splendour and squalor, with a casual sprinkling of commercial buildings of all kinds—of stone, brick, timber, wattle and daub, with roofs of tile and roofs of thatch

Newgate and part of the city wall, looking north-east towards the Cripplegate Fort.

—fine metalled roads here with stone curbs on either side, and muddy lanes there with open drains running down the centre.

Excavation has confirmed a date of AD 200, or perhaps a little earlier, during the governorship of Clodius Albinus, for the construction of the city defences. These are exactly defined by the later medieval city, except for an enlargement at the south-west corner, where the wall was extended to the banks of the Fleet in the reign of King Edward I. The existence of a Roman river wall was finally established in 1975. The north and west

sides of the 2nd-century fort were incorporated in the defences, and its two outer gates then served as entrances to the town, although the west gate was later blocked. Ludgate, Newgate, Aldersgate, the fort gates, Bishopsgate, Aldgate and, probably, Aldermanbury and Tower Posterns, were all Roman foundations. Moorgate was enlarged from a medieval postern into a gateway in 1415, and so is later.

The Roman wall varied in thickness between 2.1 and 2.8 metres and was faced with squared and coursed blocks of Kentish ragstone with a core of cemented rubble. At 0.6–0.9-metre vertical intervals there were triple bonding or levelling courses of Roman tiles, and these were carried through the wall. Wall height is estimated at more than 6 metres. Material from the shallow U-shaped ditch was used to create an internal rampart backing the wall.

Remains of the towered gateways are scanty: only at Newgate and Aldersgate are there surviving foundations of any importance, and the form of these two gates was totally different. The Newgate remains are of a simple rectangular structure, measuring 29 metres wide by 9.75 metres deep, with double gate passages. Aldersgate's sharply projecting rounded gate towers indicate a later date of construction. Like Aldersgate, Newgate was set awkwardly at an angle to the wall, so that while its northern end projected 2.1 metres, its southern end stood out fully 4.3 metres. It would have been normal for the ditch to have been spanned by a timber bridge wide enough to allow unimpeded access to the two gate passages —one for inward and the other for outward traffic.

Bastions constructed as mountings for *ballistae* were added to the outer face of the wall in late Roman times, but their number and frequency is unknown, since some excavated examples appear to be medieval.

Surprisingly little is known of the history of Roman London. Tacitus, Ammianus Marcellinus, the historian, and Ptolemy, the geographer, mention the city of their own day—the 1st–2nd century AD. It appears in the Antonine Itinerary of the early 3rd century as the focal point of the British road system. In the late 3rd century Eumenius, the private secretary to Constantius Chlorus, lets in a pinpoint of light to illumine a city desperately beset after the collapse of the short-lived British Empire. A Bishop of London attended the Council of Arles in AD 314. The *Notitia Dignitatum* of AD 300–428—a wide dating since it is a compilation—mentions the 'officer in charge of the Treasury at Augusta [London]', an indication of the financial importance of the city at that late date; and finally there are two Byzantine references to 'Lindonion' and 'Londinium Augusti'. Nothing further is recorded until the medieval chroniclers begin their fabulous legends, some of which may be far-off, distorted echoes of real historical happenings.

We know nothing of the decay of the great structures in the city, but we do know that the fortifications were energetically maintained, and this means that there was much left to defend, and the will to do so. It is now thought unlikely that the place was ever completely abandoned, but not until the bishopric was revived in 604 by St Augustine can it be said that London emerged from the shadows of Imperial Rome and within her ancient, time-scarred walls renewed herself.

London
The Cripplegate
Fort

The curious planning of the landward wall on the north-west side of the city, with its deep re-entrant between Cripplegate and Newgate, was noted by Sir Mortimer Wheeler in his Royal Commission report of 1928: 'This salient represents a skirting by the wall of a quarter already definitely laid out before the wall was built'. This deduction, from the evidence then available, was just and accurate, but not until German bombing in 1940–44 had laid bare the foundations of the Cripplegate area, could Professor Grimes brilliantly confirm and expand the deduction, and show that the presence of a pre-existent fort had there dictated the line of the city defences.

Excavations along the west wall of what proved to be the fort, first revealed unexpected differences in building methods; and particularly the absence of the bonding or levelling course of tiles, characteristic of the city wall proper. A further puzzling factor was the discovery of two thinner walls, defined by a straight joint, running parallel at this point, whose total thickness equalled that of the city wall. The inner half was

The Fort at Cripplegate
from the south.

58

clearly the later addition, since its footings had been inserted into the artificial back bank of the outer. A little further south, the outer half of this double wall was seen dramatically to swing eastwards towards the city, while the inner half stopped short at what was immediately recognised as the typical corner turret of a Roman fort: this resolved the mystery. The significance of the right-angle already established at the north-west extremity of the Roman city, by St Giles Cripplegate Church, was now grasped: the lines of the fort walls were projected, and happily confirmed in further investigations.

The Roman fort thus revealed measured about 231.6 metres from north to south, and 216.4 metres from east to west. Originally it had walls under 1.2 metres thick, with a bank internally, made of material thrown up from the V-shaped ditch, characteristic of Roman military fortification. When the city defences were built, and the fort was incorporated into them, the inner thickening wall was added to the slighter military work, to bring it up to the required width. However, this thickening only extended around the north and west sides of the fort; and the status of the fort after its incorporation remains unclear. It is possible that its south and east walls were demolished at this time, so that its area became one with the civil settlement. It seems more likely that the convenient separation of military and civilian life continued, in keeping with Roman policy: the propriety of such an arrangement is, after all, reflected in the original siting of the fort.

The intrusion of deep cellars and modern foundations into the ancient levels had effectively destroyed most internal features of the fort. However, the positions of the west and south gates were established, and then it could be seen that Wood Street, running north-south, and Addle Street and Silver Street, running east-west, perpetuate *via praetoria* and *via principalis*. Traces of barrack buildings were also uncovered, with evidence of a plain mosaic floor and fragments of wall plaster. These are unusual finds in a military base, and perhaps indicate the more lavish accommodation provided for staff officers and the like. The evidence of pottery and coins has led expert opinion to deduce a building date in the early 2nd century AD.

London
The Streets

Traces of a typical Roman grid-pattern of streets have been found in London, and the identification of this pattern has been greatly helped by the natural assumption that streets led to the gates, whose positions have been positively established; so, an approximately north by south, and east by west grid has been pieced together. But one's instinctive thought in looking back to the earliest years of the Roman occupation is that, when the legions marching up from the south came over the bridge, they would have debouched north-east and north-west as well as more directly to the north. In other words, there must surely have been an earlier diagonal pattern of roads coming from the bridge, and the typical Roman grid was superimposed on it. But there is very little surviving evidence of this rational plan, except for traces of a gravel road on timber foundations running approximately north-west, which does, indeed, exactly conform to the bridge-diagonal pattern. In its presumed direction, based on the

A typical street scene in Roman London.

evidence of building fragments found at the junction of Bread Lane and Watling Street, it tends to bend towards Ludgate rather than Newgate. To the north-east of the bridge, however, nothing has been discovered which encourages the idea of an Aldgate-bridge diagonal, so all that can be said is that, while some evidence exists for the rational diagonal plan, there is evidence also for its submergence by the grid-plan.

For the latter we have conclusive evidence. At the east end of the forum, a well-marked length of gravel road metalling 7.6 metres wide has been found, running north to Bishopsgate and Ermine Street, made up to no less than 2.4 metres in thickness, which would seem to indicate continual resurfacing over a very long period of time. To the west of the basilica and forum, indications of another north-south road have been noted. To the south, and running east-west, continuing along the line of Bucklersbury, fragments of a well-defined street, pointing to Newgate, have also been unearthed. A portion of this street was found by Sir Christopher Wren when he was digging the foundations for a new church at St Mary-le-Bow after the great fire of 1666. He reported 'a Roman Causeway of rough stone, close and well rammed with Roman Brick and Rubbish at the Bottom, for a Foundation, and all firmly cemented'. So sure was Wren of the stability of this ancient fragment that he laid the foundation of his delicate fantasy of a tower directly upon it. Some 30 metres to the west of the tower, archaeologists have picked up the line and found several superimposed roads in a deposit over 0.6 metre thick, with further traces from St Martin le Grand along Newgate Street, leading directly to the gate and the road to Silchester and the west.

Part of Cannon Street overlies an east-west element in the grid. Walbrook stream was probably bridged at two points, although no traces of

Roman wells to the west of Walbrook.

these—presumably timber—structures have survived. The streets varied in width from 5.5 to 10.7 metres. They were made with local gravel mixed with concrete which resulted in an almost rock-like hardness. They were cambered, with gullies along the sides, and flanked with paved sidewalks, which in some cases may well have been protected by colonnades. The streets were linked by a network of alleys very similar in character to those of medieval London, some of which still survive.

**London
The Governor's
Palace**

Cannon Street Station has submerged, if not obliterated, the western half of a late 1st-century complex of buildings which have been called, fancifully, but not without some rationality, the 'Governor's Palace'. The recently excavated fragments are bounded on the east by Suffolk Lane, on

the south by Upper Thames Street, and on the north by Cannon Street. In a central position on the site are the massive remains of a hall measuring 15.2 metres by 29 metres, aligned in a puzzlingly awkward way, with the longer axis north-south. To the east (and, it is presumed, to the west also), is a fragmentary apsidal structure, connected with the central hall by massive walls; the whole of this suite was probably used for official functions. To the north and south there were large courtyards enclosed by a quadrilateral of colonnaded buildings, comprising a great number of small rooms—probably administrative offices and domestic quarters— with indications of staircases suggesting an upper storey. In the south courtyard a great walled pool, with its floor 1.83 metres below the courtyard level, has been identified, with the base of what may well have been a fountain in a rounded projection on its north side—indeed, two fountains may be postulated, bearing in mind the Roman passion for symmetry in architectural form, if one assumes that beneath Cannon Street Station lies, or lay, the other complementary half of this Governor's Palace complex.

The Governor's Palace from the south.

Excavators of the site, whether they have been sewer diggers, railway engineers, or archaeologists, have commented on the enormously massive construction of the walls: one wall discovered in 1840 was 6.1–6.7 metres in width; and when the railway station was being built in 1868, 'an immense external wall', 61 metres long, 3 metres high and 3.6 metres thick, running east and west was found, together with cross walls and the remains of apartments with tessellated pavements and wall paintings. The land sloped steeply towards the river in this area, and seems to have been terraced in Roman times, but the courtyards were level, and the south courtyard was built up as a platform of 'flint and ragstone rubble concrete 1.8–2.1 metres thick' (Merrifield). Tiles have been found stamped P.P.BR.LON. (Procurator Provinciae Britanniae, Londinium), which suggests that they were used in a Government building. The Emperor Hadrian may well have stayed in this palace during his visit to Britain in AD 122.

London The Basilica and Forum

The basilica was the focal point of Roman London, physically as well as administratively. The traveller from the south, on crossing the bridge, would have seen its great bulk immediately before and above him at the top of the hill which we call Cornhill, where Leadenhall Market now stands. Over 150 metres in length, it was longer than the basilica of any other city north of the Alps. It was aligned east and west, parallel to the river, and must have towered above the surrounding buildings as did St Paul's before the construction of the hideously dreary office blocks which now disfigure the city.

The total width of the basilica was about 48.8 metres. It was aisled. The main nave—with the north aisle opening on to a double row of what were probably administrative offices and courtrooms on its north side—is shown in the drawing. Beyond the cross wall with its screen of columns is the apsidal east end, where there would have been a tribune or dais for the delivery of judgements. There is some evidence of a vaulted roof. Fragments of fresco wall decorations have been found, and we may reasonably

The basilica, interior looking east.

believe the interior to have been as rich and splendid as it was vast.

The excavated remains, however, present some confusing features: there is an unaccountable double wall extending nearly half way along the south side of the nave, and a difference in date has been detected between the various fragments that have been found in this area. It is now thought that the south aisle was open to the forum and took the form of an open arcade. This would have meant that the basilica, or a large portion of it, was in effect an extension of the forum as a meeting place and promenade. One must suppose, however, that some portion of the basilica on this side would have been completely walled—it is difficult to visualise legal and administrative processes functioning in a brisk westerly gale.

Expert opinion is now generally agreed that the basilica was built about AD 80–90, and extended westward to its full length in the early 2nd century. Evidence in the form of a thick layer of ash has been found on the site, which suggests that a fire which devastated the city in about AD 125–30 may have destroyed the earlier building and so have been the reason or excuse for the extension westwards.

The basilica summed up in one great structure all the administrative and legal functions of the state, unlike our present usage which houses law courts and government under separate roofs. In addition, it was the meeting place of the merchants, rather like the Guildhall of two hundred years ago. Its architectural form, with aisles separated from the central space by rows of columns, and with its apsidal ends, was, of course, the prototype of the early Christian churches of the west.

The London basilica occupied the north side of the great open space of the forum, and they cannot be dissociated, the one from the other: the forum might be described as the atrium or forecourt to the basilica. The three wings of the forum contained rows of shops and offices, linked and protected by a colonnaded walk. There would have been a monumental entrance in the centre of the south side, and a rostrum or altar flanked by columns crowned with gilded statues in the middle of the square. This architectural formality was qualified, no doubt, by the temporary stalls and booths set up on market days and festival days.

There is evidence that the forum in its final development dates from Hadrianic times; substantial traces of its south wall and arcade have been found along the line of Lombard Street, where it meets Gracechurch Street. That the building of this Hadrianic forum made necessary the demolition of earlier buildings of various dates has been demonstrated by the discovery of their fragmentary remains.

**London
The Walbrook
Mithraeum**

In 1952, when the bombed and rubble-covered Walbrook area, now occupied by Bucklersbury House, was due for clearance and building development, Professor Grimes, the then Director of the London Museum, supervised the cutting of exploratory trenches from east to west across the site, to establish the nature and extent of the Walbrook valley in Roman times. The channel of the stream, as excavated, was slighter than had been expected: it was only 3.6–4.3 metres wide at this point, with banks raised by artificial accumulations, which were held back by timber revetments. Nevertheless, the whole valley must have been damp, and even marshy in places, with evidence of alder and willow thickets in the earlier phases of the occupation. On the west bank, traces of buildings supported on closely driven piles were found, and a rich haul of metal, pottery and even leather and wooden objects, preserved in the wet conditions, rewarded the investigation. On the east bank, successive floor levels and a sleeper wall with settings for column bases were discovered, which the excavators judged to have belonged to a building of basilican type. Fortunately, the owners of the site and the builders were here persuaded to allow a more extensive excavation, and so the famous Walbrook Mithraeum came to light, soon to be the centre of extraordinary public interest.

The Roman levels were, for a London site, wonderfully perfect, with

Walbrook Mithraeum
from the north-west.

walls surviving to about a metre in height. The west end of the temple was within 6 metres of the Walbrook stream, and terminated in a semi-circular apse which was supported by massive square and convex buttresses. The main body of the temple was an aisled rectangle, measuring 17.8 metres by 7.9 metres, entered at its east end through a cross hall or narthex, which it was not possible to excavate. The wall construction was of Kentish ragstone, with intermittent tile courses.

The interior had undergone a long period of alterations, with nine successive floors in the nave, which had raised the level by 0.91 metre. In the first phase of the temple, which is shown in the drawing, dated to the end of the 2nd century AD, the nave was boarded, with a double step down from the narthex, and a corresponding double step up to the sanctuary at the further end, the upper and wider step here probably carrying an altar. The aisles were also at a higher level.

Beyond the altar, some evidence of a tabernacle supported by a pair of columns was found. This would have framed the sacred image of Mithras slaying the bull, which was concealed behind a screen or curtain. Towards the eastern end of the nave, there were probably two smaller tabernacles containing statues of Cautes and Cautopates, the companions of Mithras: Cautes holding a torch upwards, symbolising Day, and Cautopates with his torch downwards, Night: a fragment of the

Cautopates was found. The excavation confirmed that the nave was divided from the aisles by columns. There were seven a side, symbolising 'the seven grades into which the devotees of the cult were divided' (Grimes): these have been identified as Raven, Bridegroom, Soldier, Lion, Persian, Courier of the Sun, and Father, although their significance is not clear. In the drawing, at a critical moment in the Mithraic ritual, two devotees wearing the fantastic masks and apparel of the Raven and Lion carry flaming torches, while the Father approaches the altar. Except for the light coming from the clerestory windows, the services were conducted in a darkness tempered only by torchlight, with special effects to illuminate the Mithraic image: the deep gloom was intended to emphasise the cave-like feeling of the temple, for Mithras was said to have been 'born from the rocks', and the 'cavern' was used to signify the world.

The image of Mithras, and of other gods worshipped in the temple, had been deliberately buried, perhaps in the early 4th century, when the victorious Christians were vigorously opposing what they regarded, unjustly, as a blasphemous rival. In the upper levels, unburied, was found a marble Bacchic group, indicating that the temple remained in use for some time after this act of fear. At length, the columns themselves were removed, perhaps because of their ritualistic significance, or simply through subsidence, and the modified temple became increasingly ramshackle.

Interior of the Walbrook Mithraeum looking west: the invocation of the god.

London The Blackfriars Barge

The Blackfriars barge was first discovered—a small portion of the bows—in 1962, and in the following year another much larger portion, almost the entire afterpart of the craft, came to light in the mud to the east of Blackfriars Bridge where the Fleet river once flowed into the Thames. The discovery was made through the forming of a coffer-dam in the Thames in connection with roadworks, and this was fortunate since it meant that archaeological investigation could take place in reasonably dry conditions.

The timbers of the barge were found to have been attacked by the teredo beetle, which cannot live in fresh water, and so it is evident that this was not a river craft only, and must have sailed in the salt waters of the estuary; though its shallow build—it was 2.3 metres to the gunwales—and extremely crude construction, make it unlikely that it ever ventured

The Blackfriars Barge: the confluence of the Fleet with the Thames must have caused some difficulty in mooring.

far from the shelter of the land. Like the traditional Thames barge, it was flat-bottomed; but, unlike that fine craft, it had no keel and depended on the massiveness of its construction, rather than on skilful design, to hold it together.

It is supposed that the barge had a single mast, carrying a square sail, and the excavators found the seating for this mast forward of the open hold. In it was a worn copper coin of Domitian, the reverse bearing the image of the goddess Fortuna uppermost: she is holding a ship's rudder or steering oar, and the coin had evidently been selected for its appropriateness. There is no evidence to indicate the reason for the foundering of the barge at Blackfriars, but it is thought likely that the cargo shifted after the barge had sunk, and so the idea of a sudden, dramatic heeling-over, with the ragstone splitting its massive sides, can be discounted. Pottery found in connection with the wreck dated mainly from the 1st and 2nd centuries, and the Kentish ragstone cargo has been considered as evidence that this was one of the barges employed to bring the rough stones from the Medway for the building of the city wall, about AD 200. How many times, one wonders, did this clumsy, heavy-laden barge creep out of the Medway and drift slowly up the reaches of the Thames, negotiate the bridge, and unload its cargo? And how many such barges were involved in this great wall-building operation at Londinium?

St Albans The Roman Town

Verulamium, today St Albans, is one of those towns, of which Colchester and Silchester are important instances, with pre-Roman origins. The site of Roman Silchester coincided almost exactly with that of its Belgic predecessor, but at Colchester and St Albans the new Roman settlements grew up beside the earlier towns, and, in effect, destroyed them by absorbing their population and administrative functions. At Verulamium, the Belgic town lay to the north and north-west of the Roman site, on a plateau, known today as Prae Wood, rising from the valley of the River Ver. It was long thought that the extensive earthworks and ditches that still survive there were fragments of the *oppidum* of Cassivelaunus, which was taken by Julius Caesar in 54 BC; but Wheathampstead, 8 kilometres to the north-east, has now been more confidently identified as the scene of that engagement.

With the advance of the legions in the Claudian conquest, Watling Street was driven up and along the valley of the Ver below the Belgic settlement. The importance of the river crossing at St Michael's ford, which still exists, would have been recognised, and a fortified post may have been established to command it. What is certain is that the growth of the 1st-century town around this nucleus was rapid, for by AD 60 Verulamium had become a *municipium*, 'the highest rank which Rome could award to a native foundation', according to Tacitus. In 1955 a 1st-century defensive ditch and bank, no doubt with the usual palisade, was discovered, enclosing three sides of the town rectangle within the later walls: the fourth side, towards the river, was left open, but covered by marshy ground. The dating of these defences is a matter of some difficulty, but that they were pre-Boudiccan is considered likely. It has often been suggested that, in the uprising of AD 60, Boudicca selected Camulodunum,

Verulamium from the south-east, as it might have appeared in the late 3rd century AD.

Londinium and Verulamium as major victims for assault, because they had no defences, but this is, in fact, a misreading of Tacitus, who wrote that the Iceni avoided 'forts and military posts', which is not quite the same thing. By AD 60 the Claudian fort at Verulamium had certainly been engulfed by the new town, and its garrison evacuated.

Traces of Roman pre-Boudiccan buildings, all of timber, have been

found, notably a row of shops for bronze-workers, connected by a colonnade fronting on Watling Street. Their starkly functional design and workmanship show the hand of the military engineer, anxious to hasten the settlement of the native Britons into towns after the Roman model. But shops and timber houses, no less than the infilling of Belgic huts with their thatched roofs, only needed the Iceni torches to start an enormous, totally consuming bonfire.

After a lapse of 15–20 years of near desolation following this disaster, Verulamium was laid out anew, with the awkward diagonal of Watling Street remaining within the street grid, to give a special character to the town. To this period belong the basilica and the Romano-Celtic temple. Rebuilding on a large scale came after a serious fire in c. AD 155: the theatre and the triangular temple were now constructed, and so were many of the wealthy stone houses in the southern quarter of the town, with their delicate wall paintings and splendid mosaics. It is interesting to compare these essentially Classical—that is, stylistically Mediterranean—works with the 3rd-century, gorgeous, but crude works which have also been discovered.

The 1st-century bank and ditch of unhappy memory were levelled as the town expanded. A fresh defensive work, known as The Fosse, a portion of which has survived to the north and west outside the later town wall, was begun, perhaps in the late 2nd century, but never completed: we do not know why. The great gates across Watling Street, to the north-west and south-east of the town, may also have been built at this time, at first as isolated structures, to be incorporated into the town wall when that came into being in about AD 200. The limits of the old late Antonine town were commemorated by the erection of two monumental arches, both on Watling Street: one at a point 30.5 metres south of the triangular temple, and the other halfway between the theatre and the north-west or Chester Gate. A third monumental arch across Watling Street was built at a later date, possibly around AD 300: it was immediately adjacent to the theatre.

The 3rd century was a period of stagnancy and decline: only with the restoration of authority towards its end, did prosperity return, although changes have been noted, linked with the rise of Christianity. Nevertheless, the town prospered, and continued to do so well into the 5th century. At least one fine mansion was erected as late as AD 370, and later still, c. AD 380–90, was floored with fine new mosaics. And in the middle of the century there was still sufficient vitality—and money—to make it possible to add new-style bastions and towers to the south wall.

No other Roman town in Britain has such a well-recorded history in the 5th century. In 429 Bishop Germanus of Auxerre visited Verulamium and, according to a near-contemporary account, went in procession to the tomb of the proto-martyr St Alban, on the hilltop to the east of the city, attended by a multitude of people and magistrates and a man of tribunician rank, all in splendid apparel. He visited the town again in 447—he came to Britain on both occasions for 'religious disputation'. The good bishop was asked to lead a force against the Picts, and so he assumed command of the Britons, organised an ambush, and with the unlikely battle-cry of 'Alleluia', attacked and destroyed the barbarians at a site traditionally in the Welsh Marches.

Geoffrey of Monmouth—not perhaps the most reliable of historians—relates that Verulamium was held by the Saxons at the end of the 5th century, and that a battle was fought with the Britons, led by Uther Pendragon. By the 11th century the Roman town had become a quarry—for the emergent monastery and buildings centred on St Alban's shrine—and the ruins, according to an account preserved by Matthew Paris, were 'the hiding places of robbers, body-snatchers and evil women'. Spoliation has continued through the ages to the present day, with the construction of an arterial road across the site.

**St Albans
The Forum** The open space of the Verulamium forum measured 93 metres by 61 metres, and was contained on the north by the basilica—which an inscription tells us was completed by AD 79—and on the other three sides by ambulatories of early 2nd-century date. To east and west, the shorter sides were interrupted midway by monumental entrances to the street, one of which is shown on the right of the drawing.

The architectural complex was made the more impressive by an un-

usual feature; three temple-like structures arranged along the south side, two of which appear in the drawing. The more westerly of these, with the pyramidal roof, has been dated to the late 2nd century. It has been suggested that, because of its disproportionately heavy construction, it was designed to carry a barrel vault at least 6 metres in height. Inside there was a criss-cross of strengthening walls, and the 2.4-metre thick side walls had external square projections, which may have carried free-standing columns. Fundamentally, the plan of this unique building was square, with an extension covering the forum ambulatory, and a square-sided apsidal south end. It is considered possible, even probable, that these massive foundations indicate a podium designed to carry a towering monument such as is shown in the drawing. The forum facades of the three temples have been found to be almost exactly similar in plan, and it is reasonable to think that these buildings were harmonious in design, having Classical-type colonnades, with the usual triangular pediments and entablatures.

The open space of the forum was the equivalent to the Italian piazza or the English market-square, though the latter is seldom so concentrated or formal in design. The column surmounted by the statue of Victory has no archaeological authority in this instance, but it was not unusual to ornament public areas in this way, and there is every reason to suppose that the human activities, trading and entertainments, as shown, were normal in such a setting.

The forum from the basilica, as it might have appeared in the 2nd century AD.

St Albans
The Theatre

Few indications of Romano-British theatres have been found, and the theatre at Verulamium is the only instance where the complete plan has survived and has been excavated and recorded. Its structural history extends over a period of 250 years.

The theatre was built c. AD 155, soon after a disastrous fire had destroyed much of the town and, as no signs of earlier buildings have been found on the site, it is probable that the space had been reserved for it from the beginning. Theatres were used for religious ceremonies as well as for entertainments of all kinds. This theatre was on the same axis as, and connected with, the Romano-Celtic temple situated immediately to its south-west (extending out of the foreground of the drawing). The connection becomes clearer when the form of this First Period theatre is considered, for it bore a distinct likeness to an amphitheatre, suitable for religious processions and ceremonies. The orchestra—the central area—planned as a circular arena, was then the focal point for the audience ranged around it, rather than the stage, which was small with its front bitten back and conforming to the curve of the arena wall. Backstage there was a narrow dressing room. Sir Mortimer Wheeler has described this circular orchestra type as the 'cockpit theatre'. He notes that 20 or more examples have been found in Gaul, mostly in the north, and links them with the Gallo-Roman or Romano-Celtic temple as a 'manifestation of . . . provincial individuality'. The outer, supporting wall of the whole theatre structure was perhaps 7.6 metres high, strengthened with buttresses, and between this and the arena wall was a filling of gravel, on which were laid the wooden seats of the auditorium or *cavea*, which were

The theatre at Verulamium from the south, as it might have appeared c. AD 200.

Alan Sorrell
1967

reached by external and internal stairs. Access to the arena-orchestra was through vaulted tunnels beneath the cavea.

Very soon—c. AD 160—this cockpit theatre was altered to bring it closer to the more normal type of Roman theatre. The stage front was now straightened and the orchestra behind the cross-entrance was provided with benching, supported by massive timber uprights, where the dignitaries of the town would have sat. The stage itself was embellished with a row of Corinthian columns 5.8 metres high, and no doubt, the appropriate entablature and an architectural background and exits were provided, similar to those which are still to be seen in the theatres at Orange, Sabratha and Aspendos.

Forty years later, in c. AD 200, at the period shown in the drawing, a second wall was added along the front of the stage, leaving a slot into which the curtain would have been lowered before the performance. At either end of this slot were vertical posts with counterweights for the raising and lowering necessary: one of the counterweights has been recovered.

A period of decay followed from the middle of the 3rd century; then, about AD 296, repairs were once more put in hand. The theatre was comprehensively enlarged and the orchestra cleared, perhaps indicating a return to the shows of an earlier period. This flourishing time continued until about AD 380, after which the theatre seems to have been abandoned and used as a rubbish heap. It is remarkable that a great public building in the centre of a still prosperous town should have been treated in this contemptuous way, and it has been suggested that Christian disapproval of ritual and ceremonies connected with pagan cults may have been the cause.

St Albans The Triangular Temple

The street grid at a point 213.3 metres from the (not yet built) south-east gate of the town, impinged on the pre-existing diagonal line of Watling Street, and an awkward triangle resulted from this convergence. In the early 2nd century this important site was devoted to a temple, a structure sufficiently significant, functionally and aesthetically, for such prominence.

The shape of temple and courtyard was, inevitably, a truncated triangle, with the temple standing transversely across its broader end or base. This was divided into three compartments or cells, of which the central and most holy was a self-contained unit, separated from the other two by a wide corridor. It contained the statue of the god—the imprint of whose red and yellow painted pedestal was found by the excavator. In the two side cells were pits or tanks, centrally placed, which may have been used for burnt offerings, since oak charcoal was found in them. There were no fewer than 15 of these small pits in the floors of the temple and courtyard, all containing calcined bones of animals, oak charcoal and pottery; and in at least two of them were deposits of charred seeds and scales from cones of the Italian pine. All these, no doubt, were connected with votive offerings. The floors of the temple and converging side corridors stood 0.3 metre above the level of the courtyard, perhaps to avoid the risk of rainwater flooding.

The triangular temple from the south, as it might have appeared in the late 3rd century AD.

In the first half of the 2nd century, soon after it had been built, a serious subsidence occurred, due to the faulty filling of an underlying ditch, which had run parallel to the early Watling Street. The temple and the colonnades surrounding the courtyard were affected: probably a number of the columns had to be renewed, as well as the massive central piers on the north side which flanked the entrance to the *cella* itself. An external timber porch was added at the same time, and the high surrounding walls faced with crimson-coloured plaster.

At a distance 6.1 metres south of the porch, and on the same axis, there stood, it is supposed, a large external altar, whose chalk foundation has been found. Wooden posts, at 1.5-metre intervals along three sides of the temple complex, protected the walls from damage by waggons and wheeled traffic, and although post holes have not been found to extend as far as the altar, it is easy to imagine this part of the street being used as a gathering place for worshippers and for ceremonial use.

In a final phase, the level of both courtyard and adjacent corridors was raised, and the central altar in the courtyard was rebuilt, and flanked by two smaller pedestals. An ox skull, found buried in the floor immediately behind the central altar, is thought to have been connected with the dedication-sacrifice of the temple, following this restoration.

The nature of the votive offerings gives some clue to the dedication of the temple, and especially the pine seeds, which must have been imported from Italy at great cost. They were an offering associated with the worship of the Phrygian Cybele, the 'Great Mother', the goddess of human progress, and patroness of cities. In art she was represented wearing a diadem of towers: no site in Verulamium could have been more appropriate for her shrine.

Silchester The Roman Town

Silchester, known to the Romano-Britons as Calleva Atrebatum, lies ten miles south of modern Reading. The only visible remains of the Roman town today are remarkably well-preserved stretches of the town wall, enclosing corn fields, a medieval church, and some farm buildings. In the 19th century the whole area of the town was excavated, and a rich booty of objects of all kinds was extracted from the ground, but the architectural remains had to be re-interred as exposure to the elements was causing rapid deterioration and threatened total loss.

The town spread over an area of about 43.3 hectares. An oppidum—a defended native settlement—occupied the site before Roman times, and was the capital of the Atrebates, a Belgic tribe which had fled before the victorious Caesar from Gaul in 50 BC. The refugees assumed the rôle of conquerors in southern Britain, and gained control of a large area of Hampshire and adjacent counties. Some outlying dykes which may relate to their settlement have been found to the south-west of the later walled area.

In fact, three complete defensive systems preceded the building of the town wall. The earliest was a polygonal enclosure of about 36.4 hectares, which has been dated to about AD 43–47, and to the reign of King Cogidubnus, a native ally of the Romans. This so-called Inner Earthwork, partly underlying the walled town, may have been sanctioned by the Romans to protect the King and his people from revenge sorties of the hostile British forces of Caractacus, then being driven into the west. The Inner Earthwork appears to have gone out of use at an early date—probably as soon as the immediate threat had been removed—and to have been carefully levelled before c. AD 60.

Before the end of the 1st century a new and much larger earthwork was constructed, enclosing about 95.1 hectares including the amphitheatre. In the drawing, traces of two phases of this Outer Earthwork can be seen to the west, beyond the walled area. The regular street grid is contemporary with the Outer Earthwork, because it has been found to extend up to it, most clearly on the north and west sides. The fact that many of the public buildings—the forum and basilica, the baths (south-east of the forum), and some one hundred other structures—conflict with the street grid, as if conforming to some earlier street system, is a mystery that cannot be explained on the information at present available. The early excavators, however, found clear evidence of this conflict at the baths, where eight Tuscan columns of a fine entrance portico projecting 1.5 metres out of alignment, had been ruthlessly cut down and their stumps

Silchester from the east, as it might have appeared in the 4th century AD.

buried by a ruler-straight road which was subsequently laid. And so it would seem that things have not changed very much in historical times, and that Bumbledom and Town Planners (fatal combination) have always put 'The Scheme' before flexibility and amenity. The baths and other nearby eccentrically sited buildings were close to the banks of a stream, which supplied them with water, and coped with drainage; the stream still flows on.

Towards the end of the 2nd century the town was reduced to a more realistic size, by the construction of a new earthwork for defence, against which the wall itself was built in the early 3rd century. No turrets or bastions have been found along the wall. The four main gates opened to the north, south, east and west, the latter pair very powerful structures with guard-rooms, and towers recessed into the wall. They had double carriageways, while the north and south gates had single portals. In addition, there were three posterns.

Some twenty-five large town houses, about the same number of smaller ones, and a considerable number of shops, warehouses, workshops and industrial buildings have been excavated and, although the dating is not altogether certain, houses entirely of masonry probably only began to appear in the 2nd century. Primitive circular huts of the late 1st century have been discovered in the north-east periphery of the town, suggesting that the process of Romanisation may have been slow. A marked characteristic of Calleva appears to have been the high proportion of open space within the walls, and we can assume orchards, pasture, small holdings and courtyard gardens, although some blank areas on the plan may be attributed to the failure of 19th-century excavators to recognise timber foundations.

As at Caerwent, a large *mansio*, a public building to accommodate travellers using the Imperial Post, stood near the south gate. It was divided into suites of rooms with hypocausts and, in addition, had a commodious suite of baths with a sluice gate through the town wall to carry off water and drain the latrine. Five temples have also been found, two of them in a sacred enclosure, or *temenos*, which obstructed the central street from the forum to the east gate. Three of the temples were of Romano-Celtic type; another was polygonal in plan; and the fifth was rectangular, with an apsidal end, suggestive of a *mithraeum*. To the south-east of the basilica are the remains of what may have been a Christian church, a rarity so remarkable that it may be described as unique. The amphitheatre, served by a postern gate near the north-east angle, has not been excavated.

Calleva Atrebatum has no recorded history, but we know that the basilica was rebuilt c. AD 300, after destruction that has been related to the revolt of the usurper Allectus in 296. There is some evidence of occupation into the 6th century, but in post-Roman times the town failed to survive: perhaps the absence of a navigable river may have been crucial.

Silchester
The Christian
Church

The Christian church at Calleva was first excavated in 1892, but reopened and studied by Sir Ian Richmond in 1961. It measures some 7.3 by 12.8 metres externally, and is, therefore, very much smaller than any of the substantial houses and public buildings in the town. However, its size is altogether disproportionate to its importance, since it is the only Romano-British structure of basilican form which has been claimed as a Christian church. As such, it is completely typical: narthex or vestibule with three doors, nave with apsidal end and side aisles, and the beginnings of square-ended transepts. One strikingly different feature—to modern eyes—is its orientation: the altar here is believed to have stood at the west end, at the point of intersection of nave, apse and transepts: in the drawing, we view the building from the south-east.

On the site of the supposed altar a mosaic 'of a bold chequer pattern' was found. Like everything else at Silchester, it is, of course, once again hidden by the soil. Traces of red tessellation have been found elsewhere in the nave, and in the northern end of the narthex or vestibule: the other floor areas would have been boarded or stone flagged. On the evidence of coins found still sticking to the original floor mass of lime and mortar in the nave, it is clear that the church cannot have been built before about AD 360, that is, nearly 50 years after the promulgation of the Edict for the Toleration of the Christians by Constantine the Great in AD 313.

The Christian church at Silchester in the 4th century AD, from the south-east.

In these early Christian churches the officiating priest would have stood behind the altar facing east to celebrate mass; the singers occupied the nave; the congregation was confined to the aisles; and the catechumens, or converts who had not been baptised, stood in the narthex, watching the Christian mysteries through the doors. Sir Ian Richmond has referred to a Syrian document of the 8th century AD, which states that a Christian church should have three doors to give entry, and that on the right of this entry should be 'the place where there was a holy table where the gifts for the Eucharist could be displayed'. This could well explain the area of tessellation in the northern end of the narthex noted above; indeed, a base was found upon this, which could have supported such a table. Later, the document continues, these gifts should be taken to a room on the north side of the nave. The fact that the north transept at Silchester was cut off from the rest of the building—unlike the south transept—is clearly significant in this context.

In front of the church, within the atrium, the excavators found an area of concrete, with the tile base of a font or laver, and a pit serving a soakaway on its west side for the disposal of the baptismal water, to prevent its subsequent use for magical purposes. The Syrian document, quoted above, continues: 'Let there be a forecourt, and in the middle a house for baptistery', and some such arrangement seems to have existed at Silchester. A well on the west side of the church, in line with the axis of the building, was probably connected with it.

Comparison with the Walbrook Mithraeum shows a striking similarity between the two structures: both were basilican in form, with apsidal ends, aisles and naves. Both Christianity and Mithraism, and, indeed, the worship of Isis and Dionysus, required for their initiates a closed building, as opposed to the open Classical type; the secrecy of the Christians was, of course, one of the prime reasons for the suspicions and ultimately the cruel persecutions that they had to endure. With these likenesses in mind, it will be realised that there must be a note of caution in claiming this little building as Christian, although the evidence for it seems to be strong.

The siting of the building is extremely interesting; there was no question of its being modestly hidden away in a side street; on the contrary, it stood boldly beside the great basilica, headquarters of the civil power, and in line with the grand entrance to the forum, where stood the bronze statue of the Emperor whom all must worship. What superb arrogance! To have dared so much shows that the Christians had influential support at that time, but it was a very tiny church, and so they must have been few in number. In all country districts—even, it would seem, in cantonal capitals—the old faiths flourished longer than in more cosmopolitan centres, such as Londinium. Here, in Calleva, this church was a forward-looking gesture, an equation (at the least) of Christ and Deified Emperor.

Wroxeter Temple and Houses
(colour plate 1)

Five years after the Roman invasion and the submission of south-eastern Britain, the legions were still campaigning against their obstinate and heroic enemy Caractacus, but now in the west country, among the foothills of the Welsh mountains. In the land of the Ordovices, the British prince made his last stand. He defended a hill rising sheer from a river—probably the Severn—but was utterly defeated in the engagement and fled, leaving his wife, his daughter and his brother in the hands of the victors.

The Roman base for this decisive campaign was probably at Wroxeter, or Viroconium, to give it its ancient name: evidence for this early activity has been strengthened by the discovery of forts and temporary camps in the immediate vicinity. From about AD 56 the XIVth Legion was stationed here and later, probably, the XXth Legion. Later still, in about AD 90, after the withdrawal from Scotland, a more convenient legionary base for controlling the Welsh tribes was built at Chester: Wroxeter was superseded, and handed over to the civil authorities.

At Colchester, Gloucester and Lincoln, where former legionary bases had likewise been evacuated, *coloniae* were established; but Wroxeter became the cantonal capital of the Cornovii, an unprecedented beginning for a tribal capital in Britain. In the days of the fortress a large civil settlement had, no doubt, grown up; and now the town was dignified with the amenities that its promotion automatically carried with it: law courts and forum, public baths, drainage and water supply were all provided, and the local squirearchy would have gravitated towards it, and built themselves substantial town houses, much as they did in our county towns until comparatively recently. By the end of the 2nd century Viroconium was evidently a place of wealth and importance. Almost 81 hectares came within the circuit of its defences. The River Severn washed its western side; and a tributary stream, the Bell Brook, with deeply shelving banks, flowed through its northern section. Air photographs show a concentration of timber buildings in this northern section, leaving the much larger southern area of the town for the more important structures, including the administrative buildings and the baths.

The drawing shows some of these large structures, including a somewhat mysterious stadium-like enclosure, between whose double line of walls may once have been banks of wooden seats for spectators of whatever events took place there. Unfortunately, it has not been possible to excavate more than a portion of this intriguing feature, because of the intrusion of a modern road and erosion caused by the River Severn—which has indeed carried away part of the west side of the town. What has been recovered of the enclosure measured 43.9 metres from north to south and 57.3 metres to the west, which was as far as it could be followed.

The houses, shops and temple in the drawing flanked the main street of Viroconium. The traveller coming from the north would already have passed the basilica and forum on his right, and the public baths on his left to have reached this point. Ahead, at a distance of 120 metres, the road took a sharp turn to the right and diverged to the town gate and the bridge over the river; and in the distance, beyond the wall, it can be seen aimed at a gap in the Church Stretton hills. The buildings in the foreground were shops with living quarters at the rear, but the large building with two courtyards and an arcade facing the street, which may have sheltered shops, was perhaps a priest's house linked with the adjoining temple.

Building and rebuilding continued through the centuries on this site, and coin evidence indicates occupation from c. AD 105 to c. AD 380. Fragments of painted wall-decoration and mosaic have been found, as well as many precious small objects, all showing that wealth and even luxury were not inconsistent with the priestly life. At least two rooms were heated by hypocausts—smoke vents are indicated along their roofs—and there was a fairly extensive bath suite, the roofs of which can be seen half hidden by the trees of the further courtyard. Along the side of the street ran a water main, with side channels at a slightly higher level, branching under the houses; sluice gates before each house could be closed to divert the flow. The side channel of the building described above skirted the courtyard, flushed the latrine in the west wing, went under the stadium and finally discharged into the river 215 metres to the west.

The temple and its associated buildings were erected after an extensive fire in c. AD 160, when many timber buildings along the street were destroyed. It appears to have been of the usual Romano-Celtic type, with a nearly square high *cella* surrounded by a portico with a lean-to roof, set in an arcaded courtyard. There is some evidence that the temple was linked with a horse cult, in which case there may well have been a connection with the nearby stadium, where, it is reasonable to think, displays involving horses would have taken place.

**Wroxeter
The Baths**

This great bath complex occupied an entire *insula*, measuring 88.4 metres by 134.1 metres, in a central position in the town, immediately to the east of the basilica and forum, across the main north-south street. When the town was first laid out, the position of these two great blocks of public buildings was reversed: an unfinished bath suite has been found under the later forum, and the structure on the north side of the group shown in the drawing is believed to have been designed originally as the basilica for a basilica-and-forum complex. Perhaps the Britons here resisted a too hasty attempt at Romanisation. Both sites were allowed to decay after this abortive beginning, until the Hadrianic revival, when a forum and basilica were finally built on the west side of the street, c. AD 129. When the great aisled hall shown in the drawing was finally completed in the

latter part of the 2nd century, its function had changed and it became the *palaestra* or exercise hall of the grandiose bath establishment which began to come into use at this time. Its roof is remarkable, for exercise yards were usually left open to the sky, at least when the Roman conception of the 'bath suite' was first introduced to Britain; and so Wroxeter is important evidence of the early victory of the British climate over the intruding foreigner with his new ideas. However, it must be admitted that at Wroxeter, where there is so much inconclusive attribution of purpose, the roof may well have been in existence at an earlier date.

There were two entrances to the baths from the street. One was an alley, leading between a small colonnaded market hall, in the foreground of the drawing, and a range which included a large latrine (this building is shown with louvres on the roof ridge). The other, the main public entrance, was through the west wall of the *palaestra*. At the eastern end of this building were changing rooms with lockers, and from floor sweepings and animal bones found by excavators, it would seem that eating—and presumably drinking—were included in the entertainment offered by the establishment.

The baths proper occupied the eastern side of the open courtyard. Large double doors in the south wall of the *palaestra* opened into the *frigidarium* (or cold room), shown with a tiled roof. This was flanked to east and west by cold plunge baths, where the bathers could cool themselves after working up a sweat with games and exercises in the *palaestra*. From the *frigidarium*, they could choose to proceed either to one of the *laconica* (providing dry heat) or to the *tepidarium* (providing wet, tepid heat) and thence to the *caldarium* (or hot room). The small square building with the domed vault in the drawing was the western *laconicum*: another, exactly the same in all respects, was placed symmetrically on the east side of the range.

The *tepidarium* and *caldarium* were contained in the massively vaulted area. Underfloor heating circulated from the furnace at the south end, and rose through flues in the walls. Water was heated in a boiler above the furnace, and piped into the hot baths which projected from the wall of the *caldarium*. There was a special baths supply aqueduct, probably of timber construction, diverted from the main aqueduct that entered the town to the north-east of the baths.

To complete his progress through the system, the bather would return through the various chambers, allowing his body to cool gradually, and end with a cold plunge, or perhaps by running out into the courtyard where stood a *piscina* or ornamental open air pool. This pool is the most remarkable discovery at the site in recent years, and is as yet unique in Britain; but it is a provincial, faraway echo of the arcaded Canopus canal at Hadrian's Villa at Tivoli.

Soon after the bath block had been built, it began to settle into the soft, sandy subsoil, in spite of its massive foundations, and so, to prevent further trouble, a retaining wall (shown in the drawing) was constructed to a height of 1.8 metres around its three sides. A more radical change occurred c. AD 210, when a smaller bath suite was built right across the courtyard from the *frigidarium*, blocking access to the *piscina*, which was then filled with town rubbish, including masses of broken pottery, which

The Baths at Wroxeter, as they might have appeared in the 2nd century AD: looking north.

has helped to establish the date of this change of plan.

The baths ceased to function c. AD 300, and the building was probably converted into tenements in the 4th century. The *palaestra* was totally demolished and large timber buildings were erected on the site: these give a clue to the later history of the town. A massive decline in population by about AD 460 has been postulated, leading to migration to a smaller, more easily defended site, perhaps to Shrewsbury, in a loop of the river, 8 kilometres to the north-west. Only one length of walling of the old town survived above ground in the succeeding centuries when the stone robbers had finished their work: the north wall of the *frigidarium* of the baths, a miraculous survival. It stands now in the midst of cornfields, and has been known for centuries as 'The Old Work'.

Caerwent The Roman Town

Caerwent (Venta Silurum) was the capital of the Silures. They were the most hostile of all the native tribes to Roman penetration and, in consequence, were heavily garrisoned, with the IInd Legion permanently based at Caerleon (Isca Silurum), in the heart of their territory, after AD 74. The conditions were not propitious for civil development. Caerwent itself, 11 kilometres to the east of the legionary fortress, probably began as an auxiliary fort, and did not achieve civil status until the early 2nd century. Even then it only extended to 18 hectares, although its position on the main road from Gloucester to Caerleon meant that it must always have been in touch with great events.

Roughly rectangular in plan, Caerwent was bisected by the main east-west road, and divided into two rows of five *insulae*, or blocks of building, each about 85 metres square. The regularity of the layout suggests military planning, which is not inconsistent with its situation. An embankment 12.2 metres wide was thrown up round the town, probably at the end of the 2nd century, which was reinforced with a stone wall in the early 3rd century, with two ditches to give additional security. A feature of this wall, which is also to be found at Silchester, is the provision of internal projections or counterforts at intervals of about 61 metres, thought to have provided support for wooden stairways to the wall walk. There were no turrets, but bastions of an unusual polygonal design were added to both south and north walls, c. AD 330–40, as recent excavations have confirmed. A number of these, and the wall itself, survive in excellent condition.

The central block on the north side of the main street was occupied by a basilica-and-forum complex of the normal type, with the public baths across the street. Immediately to the east of the forum stood a Romano-Celtic temple with a *cella* 5.8 metres square internally, and an apse on its north side, surrounded by a portico supported by columns. It stood in a courtyard, with a vestibule fronting on to the street. This religious establishment is also thought to have included shops selling votive objects, and a detached priest's house behind. In the background of the drawing can be seen a late addition to the town, an amphitheatre that, unusually, was built inside the town walls. This was no elaborate structure, with banked seats, but an oval enclosure constructed over levelled houses and a street, with a low wall around it.

The *insula* immediately to the west of the forum contained a number of houses, some of which were excavated in 1947–48. These are shown in the second drawing. The courtyard house in the foreground (known as XXVIN) began as two simple strip-houses, each 22.56 metres long and 6.1 metres wide, with shops on the short sides facing the street, and living rooms and storage space at the back. The two houses were but 1.5 metres apart. About the middle of the 2nd century the eastern one was demolished, and an extension was built on to the back of the surviving house, at right-angles to it. Later, the eastern wing was rebuilt, at a distance, as shown in the drawing. Thus, a courtyard house was created, with an impressive colonnade projecting 3.1 metres into the street. These changes were probably not completed until the early 3rd century or later. All these houses had heated rooms with tessellated pavements. It is not known whether the walls were of stone construction throughout, or timber-framed on dwarf stone walls, but in the drawing the latter is shown as the more probable. The roofs were stone-tiled, and inside walls were plastered and painted. The stone flags along the street edge conceal a drainage channel.

Caerwent fell into decay by the end of the 4th century, and evidence of this was found during the excavation of these houses. In House XXVIN, for instance, which was already in ruins, squatters took possession, and dug a hole through the mosaic pavement for an iron-smelting pit. Later still, the north and south gates of the town, which had single portals, were

87

Roman houses and shops at Caerwent, from the south.

crudely blocked, with stones taken from buildings or tomb monuments. It is doubtful if the town was occupied beyond the beginning of the 5th century. After this we know nothing until the coming of the Normans in 1070. Modern Caerwent is built over Venta Silurum, and its main street is the old Roman road.

Bath
The Baths and Temple of Sulis Minerva
(colour plate 2)

Bath, or Aquae Sulis, has been described as the 'most sophisticated town in Roman Britain', and this sophistication was the result of the attractive power of the hot springs, with their medicinal properties. In the Roman world of the 2nd and 3rd centuries, fashionable society came to Aquae Sulis to be cured of real or fancied ills, just as it was to come in the 18th and 19th centuries. There was, however, one important difference: the Roman visitors not only bathed in the sacred waters but worshipped in the temple of the presiding deity, Sulis Minerva; in the Bath of Beau Nash the waters were scarcely looked upon as sacred, and one might say that the temperature of religion, unlike that of the hot spring, had fallen considerably.

The deity worshipped was a combination of the Celtic god Sul (Romanised as Sulis) and the Roman goddess Minerva; and this mingling of masculine and feminine, of native and partly assimilated Roman culture, is expressed in surviving fragments of the pediment of the temple, with its fiercely moustachioed gorgon's head, borne aloft by two winged Victories.

The temple stood in its sacred enclosure on the north side of the bath complex, in the very centre of the little town. To its east, on the same axis, substantial remains of what may well have been a theatre have been discovered, where, no doubt, religious ceremonies were performed, as at Verulamium. The architectural form of the temple itself was wholly Classical, with four fluted Corinthian columns and a portico, two columns deep at the east end, and a *cella* with five attached columns occupying the whole width of the podium: it has been compared with the Temple of Fortuna Virilis in Rome. The precinct (or, more properly, *temenos*) was entered from the eastern end, through a two-arched monumental gateway, and the visitor would immediately have been confronted by a large altar standing before the temple, with two statues on its west side. The base of one of these was found during excavations in 1965, with an inscription indicating that it was the gift of one Lucius Marcius Memor, augurer or soothsayer of the temple. The temple and the altar were further protected from casual promenaders by an inner, free-standing colonnade.

To the left of the gateway a massive buttressed wall, supporting a huge vault, contained the pool or reservoir of the hot spring, which was incorporated in the sacred enclosure of the temple. At the entrance, it is reasonable to suppose, stood a structure with a central doorway, known to us as the Facade of the Four Seasons, perhaps surmounted by the Luna Pediment, of which three fragments were found in 1790. This doorway might well have formed the entrance to the vaulted area, where an observation platform supported by columns may have been situated.

The dominant feature of the great complex must always have been the vault of the Great Bath, extending east and west. Here the hot spring water was directly piped, having cooled sufficiently to make it suitable for bathing. The cross vault immediately to its left covered another swimming bath, which received the outflow of the Great Bath, with a consequent further reduction in temperature. An elaborate system for the disposal of the waste water, with an outlet into the River Avon, has been discovered, much of it intact, and part of it is in use today. The lesser vaults at the east and west ends of the complex covered two separate suites—presumably for male and female bathers—of hot, tepid and cold baths of the conventional Roman type. These were artificially heated with hypocausts and independent stoking arrangements. The vault immediately to the right of the Great Bath contained the large Circular or Cold Bath, which was rather awkwardly inserted into what originally had been a spacious entrance hall. The lesser rectangular and semi-circular projections from the side wall of the Great Bath, contained alcoves for onlookers.

When first built, the artificially heated baths only were roofed with masonry, to counter the risk of fire presented by sparks flying from their furnaces. The swimming baths were probably roofed with tiles, supported by a timber structure similar to the normal basilican pattern, with aisles at a lower level. Soon, however, the steam from the hot thermal waters began to twist the beams and endanger their stability. Therefore, the series of massive vaults were constructed, as shown in the drawing, and, although box tiles were used for lightness, all the supporting walls and columns had to be strengthened to bear the increased load.

A more intractable problem arose at a later date, when a dramatic rise in the water table led to continual flooding of the hypocausts. Several times in the 4th century the floors were raised, but eventually the rising flood waters began to weaken the massive foundations, culminating, in the late 4th century, in the abandonment of the complex. At length, the enormous vaults collapsed into what had become a marsh, into which the famous spring continued to pour its hot, radioactive waters.

Little is known of the other structures of this little town because much of the modern city is sacrosanct and not available for excavation. The walls were probably in being by the end of the 2nd century. Lodging houses and inns must have been a special feature, and the richness of the surrounding country is attested by the fact that no fewer than 30 villas have been discovered within a 16-kilometre radius. Certainly, Aquae Sulis outlasted the ruin of its main attraction, and even in the early 5th century substantial stone houses were being built on the higher ground. In 577 a serious blow was struck, when the Saxons defeated the forces of the Britons at the battle of Dyrham, and the town passed into their hands; but occupation of the site continued, and it was the scene in 973 of the coronation of King Edgar.

Llantwit Major Roman Villa
South Glamorgan

This extensive villa site in Glamorgan lies 24 kilometres west-south-west of Cardiff, and just north of the village of Llantwit Major. This was the tribal territory of the Silures, which the Romans regarded as border country, and so the villa represents a remarkable intrusion of stylish country living into a garrisoned area, where villas were normally few and far between. No defences as such were provided; the bank and ditches enclosing the buildings were probably only to keep stock from wandering, and to ensure privacy.

The site (which is now turfed over again) was investigated before and after the last war by Dr V. E. Nash-Williams, who concluded that the whole villa was basically of one build, and dated from the middle of the 2nd century. More recently, in the light of further research and excavations, a more complex structural history has been proposed. An early timber villa on the site is now suspected, although its plan has not been recovered, preceded by a native settlement of some kind. The first building in stone may indeed have belonged to the mid-2nd century, but this would probably have been no more than a modest farmhouse, a simple rectangular block of rooms with no corridor. A period of severe decline and possibly even of abandonment followed in the early 3rd century, and the villa did not arrive at its characteristic L-shaped form until at least a hundred years later, c. AD 270, when the bath suite may have been built. The outbuildings are dated to c. AD 300, and the villa is now thought to have reached its period of maximum prosperity, c. AD 340–50, with the insertion of mosaic pavements and a general refurbishing. The later history of the house is less certainly dated: there is good evidence that the baths were blocked up, and their furnace used for iron-working, at some time late in the 4th century, when the family had presumably left; but it is not known when occupation finally ceased.

The drawing shows the villa at the height of its prosperity. In the foreground, the outbuildings around the outer court can be seen, comprising barns and stables and a basilican building, which may have provided accommodation for servants. On the same alignment as the basilican building, at the northern end of the outer court, a long low structure housed the estate workshops. This was connected to a narrow line of rooms with three openings on to the yard; these also served as workshops at a later date. All the outbuildings are shown roofed with slabs of the local Pennant sandstone, while the roofs of the villa proper are tiled: this

Llantwit Major: the Roman villa from the east, at the height of its prosperity.

conforms to the evidence available. The walls were of limestone or sand-stone, in some cases rendered with a hard white mortar; and Bath stone was used for decorative features.

The extension at the nearer end of the northern range contained two large reception rooms, interconnected with a wide opening. Here fragmentary mosaic pavements were found, with complicated geometric designs. On the walls traces of two coats of painted wall-plaster were found, as also in the corridor and parts of the western range. The remaining rooms were not clearly identified, but were probably a dining room, domestic shrine, kitchen and service area.

The western range contained sleeping quarters with, possibly, an upper storey and, to the south, the usual bath suite, with evidence of bright wall-painting in all its rooms. The furnace occupied the lean-to at the end of the range.

The excavator noted the sparsity of Samian ware and window glass at Llantwit, which would seem to confirm that the accommodation was not as lavish as in the villas of the civil province to the south and east.

Lullingstone Roman Villa
Kent
(colour plate 3)

This was a small house, but richly decorated, and full of associations and survivals. For over 300 years the site was occupied, altered, abandoned, re-occupied, extended, each owner leaving the stamp of his personality on the place, so that even in the ruins, traces of these several characters survive to be read. The drawing shows the probable appearance of the villa in about AD 360.

The site was a low terrace cut into the hillside, overlooking the River Darent in Kent. A Belgic farm of wood, daub and thatch stood here in pre-Roman times. In the late 1st century, the native owner had his house rebuilt in Roman style, and in more durable materials, with walls of flint and mortar. It was of a compact rectangular design: a verandah at the front towards the river was contained at either end by rooms jutting from a central range of rooms, with a narrow corridor along the back. The roof was probably thatched. The small circular temple on the higher terrace also dates from the occupation of this man or his descendants and was probably dedicated to a woodland deity.

Towards the end of the 2nd century, the house passed into other hands. To the south, an entire bath suite was added, for by this date civilised life would not have seemed complete without the cheerful, steamy, splashy atmosphere of the baths. In the drawing, the vaulted roofs of the *caldarium* and of the projecting hot bath can be distinguished, with the *frigidarium* and *tepidarium* to the right, and the furnace in continuation of the *caldarium* to the west.

At the north end of the house, no less necessary provision was made at this time for religious observance. The jutting room already in existence at this end had previously been used as a cellar for storage, since its floor was 2.4 metres below the surrounding levels. Now it was converted into a cult room for worship of the local water goddesses, the protectors of the spring, which welled up in a tank in the floor. Other cult rooms were added, to be demolished later; all were decorated with wall-paintings.

This owner was of Roman ancestry, wealthy and with refined tastes, but he appears to have abandoned the house suddenly and unexpectedly in about AD 200, leaving many valuable heirlooms behind. Since there are no signs of destruction to explain his hasty departure, it is suggested that he may have been implicated in the rebellion of Clodius Albinus, and fled the country at the reversal of the governor's fortunes. The house stood empty, and sank into decay.

When it was re-occupied in the late 3rd century, the newcomers found two ancestral portrait busts left behind by the previous occupants long before, and set them up in superstitious awe in the Deep Room, which was now sealed off for their worship. The other cult rooms at the north end of the house were in ruins; and so were taken down, and replaced by a narrow wing projecting towards the river, which is shown in the drawing. The baths were also reconstructed, but these repairs were sparingly done. A granary 24.4 metres long by 10.7 metres wide was erected by the river to store the produce of the estate. From the evidence, the newcomers were Romano-Britons, farming on a large scale. The temple-mausoleum behind the house was built some twenty years later, c. AD 300, and hints at a family tragedy, for here the bodies of a young man and woman in their twenties were found, laid to rest in coffins enclosed by a wooden sarcophagus, over which the chalk and gravel floor of the shrine had been directly laid. They were, perhaps, victims of a plague epidemic; and their memory was perpetuated in prayers said in the chapel above.

The house grew more luxurious in the 4th century, with the building of a lofty reception room and dining room in the replanned central area. It might even be said that the additions outgrew the house, since the apsidal dining room, which was very solidly built with walls of flint, burst through the back corridor of the house, dividing it into two short lengths. The changes drastically reduced space for accommodation, especially since an open courtyard was formed out of several rooms to the south of the reception rooms. Fine mosaic floors were laid in the new suite, but these were not provided with underfloor heating. All these factors suggest that after about AD 360, when these changes were complete, the house ceased to be continuously occupied, and had declined to the status of a summer lodge or retreat for its wealthy owner.

A Christian house church was established at the villa soon after, in the room above the Deep Room, while pagan worship continued below. The reconstruction of the fallen wall-paintings from the Christian rooms is one of the great achievements of recent British archaeology. This part of the house was made self-contained, with an exterior door, so that, even when the owner was away, local Christians could come in to worship.

In about AD 380 the baths were pulled down and filled in: after this, continuous occupation of the villa probably ceased. The floor of the temple-mausoleum subsided, and the graves were robbed; the granary beside the river was levelled to the ground. At length, only the Christian chapel seems to have remained in use. In the early 5th century this and the rest of the house disappeared in a blaze of destruction.

Brochs and Vikings

Clickhimin Broch
Shetland

In the north mainland of Scotland, in Orkney, Shetland and the Western Isles, many hundreds of broch sites have been discovered, all showing a remarkable similarity in plan. Material recovered from excavations suggests that a close federation of small powers in the far north, centred on Orkney, was successfully raising these unique structures, evidently for defence, in the period 1st century BC–1st century AD. Their enemies were probably the warlike tribes of central and western Scotland, whose fierce energies were turned south at the first advent of Roman arms into Scotland. The danger past, the brochs were soon abandoned—certainly by the end of the 1st century AD the population had reverted to an easier mode of life. Nevertheless, old hostilities survived, and the far north was never open to Roman civilisation. Instead, centuries later, it was the Vikings coming 'west-over-sea', first as raiders and then to settle, who exercised the decisive cultural influence in these regions.

Two broch sites in Shetland, skilfully excavated in recent years, have conclusively established dates and chronology, and yielded successive levels of occupation extending over an immense span of years.

Clickhimin: Late Bronze Age farmstead, from the south.

Clickhimin: interior of Iron Age fort with blockhouse and wall ranges.

Clickhimin, 1.2 kilometres from Lerwick, was inhabited for over 1,000 years. The first settlers on the islet, in what was originally a sea loch, were farmers of the late Bronze Age. They constructed a small, round farmstead, with an outhouse for stores, and encircled the whole with a low wall, leaving space enough to house livestock and stack peat, driftwood and hay. The islet was cut off except at low tide, when a sandy promontory linked it to the shore. Grazing would have been along the shores of the loch.

The site was taken over by early Iron Age settlers, who built their own round hut, retaining and adapting the earlier farmstead. Their successors, in the 5th–4th centuries BC, then fortified the existing arrangements. The farm-yard wall was converted into a defensive ringwork with a parapet walk, in all about 2.9 metres high, and inside the entrance was placed a strong stone blockhouse, possibly the residence of the chieftain of the clan. Other living quarters were in ranges against the fort wall to east and west: these had cattle stalls and workshops on the ground floor, and doors from the first floor gave access to the parapet walk.

The blockhouse at this period was an extraordinary building. It was three storeys high, with a front entrance at ground level, secured by a heavy wooden door, which led into a central passage with side cells. A rear entrance to the first floor of the attached accommodation was probably reached by ladder. The wall walk in the upper level of the blockhouse was contained in the thickness of the wall. The excavator has argued convincingly that this sophisticated building belongs to a stage in the evolution of the later brochs—which were built to the same principle, only carried into the round and raised to a greater height to afford more secure protection. The Iron Age forts of southern Britain are thought to have developed multivallate defences, to counter the use of slings, and brochs may well have been raised primarily to protect their vulnerable domestic ranges from the enemy's firebrands.

95

Clickhimin Broch from
the south-west.

At some time in the late Iron Age, Clickhimin Loch became land-locked, the water level rose, and the islet was permanently cut off from the shore. There was serious flooding, and the inhabitants were forced to abandon the wall ranges and blockhouse and retreat to the older structures on higher ground. A breakwater was provided to strengthen the damaged west wall, the entrance was raised about a metre and a hornwork added, and a landing stage was also constructed.

Work had begun on an inner ring wall on the higher ground, when skilled broch-builders of the fully evolved tradition arrived at Clickhimin, perhaps from Orkney, in about the 1st century BC. The new work was then abandoned, but on its foundations a broch of imposing dimensions began to rise, with walls at ground level up to 6.1 metres thick. The entrance was on the west side: a passage 5.2 metres long led into a central courtyard open to the sky, around which timber ranges two or three storeys high were built with a central hearth. The walls of the tower were solid to the first floor and rubble-filled, with two mural chambers; above this, they divided into an inner and outer casement wall, bonded together by stone-flagged galleries, through which a staircase rose to the wall walk, at a height estimated at 12–15 metres. There was probably a sloping protective roof over the wall walk.

In the drawing on this page the broch is shown complete, with the

1 Romano-Celtic temple and houses at Wroxeter in the 3rd century AD, looking west.

2 The baths and temple of Sulis Minerva from the north, as they might have appeared in the 3rd century AD.

blockhouse modified and returned to use. The circular ruin of the Bronze Age farmstead is in the background. The line of stone piers inside the western wall marks the remains of the western wall range of the first fort.

In about the 2nd century AD the upper levels of the broch were taken down, and a large wheelhouse built in the interior. This was inhabited peacefully as a farm until about the 6th century, when occupation seems to have come to an end.

Jarlshof Late Iron Age Settlement
Shetland

The name 'Jarlshof' was bestowed by Sir Walter Scott, in his novel *The Pirate*, upon the 17th-century laird's house, whose ruins dominate the excavated remains of Bronze Age, Iron Age and Viking villages at a site 1.6 kilometres north of Sumburgh Head, the southernmost tip of Shetland. The scene today is one of desolate grandeur, with the gigantic mass of Sumburgh Head, and Fair Isle on the southern horizon. The shores of the Voe, or Bay, of Sumburgh, on whose brink stand these ancient ruins, are of jagged rock, but this has not prevented erosion by the sea, and fully half of the broch and courtyard shown in the drawing have been so destroyed.

Erosion has destroyed, but blown sand has conserved Jarlshof. The drifting dunes engulfed each succeeding settlement, and a huge mound of abandoned levels of occupation gradually accumulated. Upon the crest

Late Iron Age settlement at Jarlshof from the north, as it might have appeared about 450 AD.

of this the laird's house was built, and it was not until the uncovering effected by violent storms at the end of the 19th century, that the presence of earlier villages was suspected.

As at Clickhimin, the broch tower at Jarlshof was abandoned for defensive purposes at a comparatively early date. The inhabitants, who were peaceable farmers and fishermen, then moved into the attached courtyard, and built a large round house on its landward side. The ruins of this so-called 'aisled house' can be seen in the drawing, adjoining the base of the broch: there was also a byre for the cattle, but this was destroyed by the later buildings.

In the 2nd–3rd centuries AD, new settlers arrived at Jarlshof and built the first 'wheel-house' in the centre of the courtyard. The earlier structure was modified and continued in use, reached by a stone-roofed passage that echoes the curve of the enclosure wall. The name 'wheel-house' aptly describes the internal plan of the new dwelling, for, from the central hearth space, dividing walls radiated like the spokes of a wheel. These walls isolated what were probably sleeping compartments, opening towards the fire, and carried a peripheral roof of stone slabs, sealed with turves against the weather. There were no windows, and light came from the eye above the hearth, supplemented by small stone hand lamps.

The original entrance and whole western end of this wheel-house was blocked at a later date, presumably because of the danger of rocks falling from the half-dismantled tower; and the house contracted behind a partition wall, with a new doorway opening to the south.

The three wheel-houses in the background are conjectural, but it is to be presumed that the courtyard was well built up by the time that the wheel-house in the foreground was built, for this broke through the enclosure wall, as if all other available space had been exhausted. It also entirely blocked the passage to the 'aisled house' noted above, which now went out of use.

The community continued to expand after the period shown in the drawing, and a further wheel-house was built inside the broch tower itself, and another outside the walls. In the last stages of the occupation, when the sand was piling up to 3.1 metres on the northern side of the enclosure, an earth house, something very like a rabbit burrow, was contrived in it. Other wretched huts at a distance were undoubtedly still inhabited at the time of the coming of the Vikings, and the descendants of the earlier inhabitants may well have lived on as servants of the newcomers.

Jarlshof Viking Settlement When the Vikings arrived at Jarlshof, probably in the early 9th century, they avoided the ancient settlement, and built their earliest farmstead higher up the shore. This lay roughly east-west, a two-roomed house some 21 metres long, its walls slightly bowed, with a cross passage dividing the kitchen from the living room. In the drawing, which shows the settlement as it might have appeared in about 1100, this is still the dominant house in the group, and by that date had further expanded, with a byre, approached by a cattle road, attached to its east end.

The principles of construction employed in this first homestead were common to all the later houses on this site: thick turf and stone walls

Jarlshof Viking settlement from the north, as it might have appeared in about 1100 AD.

supported a roof of turf and straw, laid on horizontal laths over the beams, and held down with weighted ropes—the form became the pattern for the Highland croft. Internally, the roof was carried on timber uprights, dividing the living space into a narrow central area with side aisles. The floors of the side aisles were raised into lateral platforms of earth, retained by stone kerbing, for table, benches and bed in the living room. Both kitchen and living room had long rectangular stone troughs for fires occupying their central space, with corresponding openings in the roof.

In the mid-9th and early 10th centuries, secondary farmsteads were built at right angles to the original house on the landward slope, probably for sons of the house. These were confined within yard walls, which rigidly defined their territorial limits. The outhouses of the parent farmstead—consisting originally of a barn, byre, smithy and stables—were in a group on the further side of a stone path leading obliquely to the farmstead. However, as the drawing shows, these arrangements were later modified. In the 11th century the secondary farms were abandoned: on the floor space of one, semi-circular cattle compounds were built; and the other contracted in length, and a cattle road was inserted into its north end, suggesting that it had been converted into a byre. Still later, lesser outhouses were built along the north side of the parent farmstead.

The inhabitants of the secondary farmsteads apparently abandoned them in favour of the group of outhouses mentioned above, which they

Interior of Viking farmstead.

converted into homes, with no intervening yard walls. While the parent house continued as a prosperous farm, these other settlers seem to have turned to fishing as their primary occupation.

Occupation continued in the 12th century, but by the end of the 13th century the settlement had declined to a single farm. In the late 16th century, this was superseded by the 'New Hall', which in turn gave place to the laird's house on the crest of the mound.

In the earliest period, the bay would have served as a convenient anchorage for boats raiding to the south, and the boats' crews may well have camped on the slope towards the shore, where traces of their fires have been found. Some loot certainly reached the settlement, but few weapons were found, and the settlers were probably self-supporting and lived in comparative peace. Field implements, loom weights, elaborate pins and combs were among the finds, and indicate a range of activities. The most exciting find was of a number of slate and sandstone tablets, with incised drawings of Viking ships, a dragon prow, and simple portraits of members of the settlement.

Saxon and Dark Ages

Cheddar Saxon Palace
Somerset

The drawing shows the royal buildings at Cheddar, as they might have appeared in the 10th century AD. In the distance are the scrub-covered Mendip Hills, wooded on the lower slopes, with the cleft of Cheddar Gorge on the left, 1.61 kilometres away. The River Yeo rises here and flows south beyond the distant monastery buildings and the site of a Roman villa, near where the parish church now stands. Thereafter it resumes a more westerly course, and deepens and becomes navigable, meandering to the Bristol Channel. The flat-bottomed storm-water ditch on the left of the drawing drained into this river 275 metres to the south-west of the palace site.

In the 9th century, in the time of Alfred, the ground was occupied by a long hall with opposite entrances midway along its bowed side walls. Other lesser rectangular buildings, all of wood, stood nearby, but these and the hall were soon abandoned and demolished. The drawing shows structures which probably date from a major reconstruction of the site before AD 941, when the Witan, the Saxon national assembly, met at Cheddar.

At the east end of the 0.81-hectare site, the excavators uncovered indications of an area fence and ditch, pierced by an entrance gate, with a well-constructed post hole just beyond. This latter was interpreted as the socket for a flagstaff carrying a banner, or for a carved wooden pillar. Immediately opposite the entrance, inside the enclosure, was the new hall, on a different alignment from its predecessor, lying east-west, with doors in its end walls. It measured 18.3 metres by 8.5–9.1 metres, and was of massive timber construction, straight-walled, with posts up to 0.6 metre square, set in pits at 2.4-metre intervals. It is thought that these posts were linked by ground timbers supporting plank walls, carrying a roof of shingles. The interior would have been lit by side windows. There was an internal porch at the west end.

To the right of the hall, in the drawing, a field-kitchen is shown, with smoke rising. The small structure opposite the west door of the hall was probably the latrine building. To the left of the hall in the drawing is the lord's private chapel, the only building in stone on the site at this date. The walls were of limestone rubble, thickly coated with cream stucco on which joint lines were painted to simulate squared stonework. The windows and doorways were of freestone.

The small wooden building near the ditch replaced an earlier building of similar size and function and, like its predecessor, was probably the 'bower' or private building for the women: internal post holes may indicate where looms were set up.

In the foreground are three linked buildings with walls of wattle and daub. The central structure was circular, with a trodden track around a central platform: this was probably a corn-mill, with mill stones set in a wooden framework, turned by human or animal power. However, no mill stones were found. The small rectangular building to its right contained an oven, and is interpreted as a bakery. Its twin on the other side of the mill may have been a grain store.

The Witan met at Cheddar in 941, 956 and 968. In the early 11th century, probably in the reign of Ethelred II, the chapel was enlarged, and the hall modified and slightly reduced. After the Norman Conquest the site still remained in favour. Henry I had a substantially larger hall built, overlying the former eastern entrance, and the smaller hall was reconstructed. Further work was undertaken in the reign of King John,

Saxon Palace at Cheddar from the west, as it might have appeared in the 10th century AD.

by which time, however, the palace had degenerated to little more than a hunting-box. John gave it away, at length, to the dean and chapter of Wells, who rebuilt the larger of the halls in stone. By the 17th century all but the chapel had fallen into ruin: this was converted into a house, and survived. The lost palace was relocated and excavated in 1960–62, under the direction of Dr P. A. Rahtz.

Thetford Saxon Houses
Norfolk

Thetford in late Saxon times had a population estimated at between four and five thousand, and ranked among the six most important towns in England. It was a market centre for wool, pottery and metal goods, and probably traded with the Continent, by way of the Little Ouse, on the south bank of which river the town stood. In Domesday Book, no fewer than 13 churches are recorded within the borough, and a mint had been established by the 10th century, and a substantial bank and ditch defended the town, terminating at either end on the river. Thetford was not a Roman foundation, and probably only began to flourish as a town after the Danish occupation and settlement in AD 870.

Excavations in 1948–52 uncovered a large industrial and artisan quarter along the western periphery of the Saxon town, inside the defences. Three superimposed roads of rammed flint were detected, with accompanying occupation levels, overlying earlier ditches, pits and huts. In the drawing, the period of the intermediate road, probably dating from the late 10th century, is shown.

In the foreground is a boat-shaped house, known as Hut 13, which was about 15.2 metres long and 4.3 metres wide at the broadest point: it is somewhat reminiscent of the first farmstead at Jarlshof, although that, of course, was built in stone. Here the walls were of horizontally laid timbers, with uprights at about 3.1-metre intervals. The roof is shown thatched. The hearth was not centrally placed, but was close against the eastern wall of the house. There was a door in the gable end.

Beyond the house, and extending far beyond the area shown in the drawing, the excavator found a thick layer of greyish ash, flecked with burnt wood, with lumps of iron slag intermixed—a clear indication of iron workings. The raw material would seem to have been dug out of the sand in the form of iron-stone pebbles, which were mixed with charcoal and roasted in fires. This activity is shown in the drawing. Bellows were used to increase the heat of the fire, but the yield of iron would not have been good: at a similar site in the north of the county, it has been estimated that 250 kilogrammes of iron-bearing pebbles would have produced only about 60 kilogrammes of ore. The laborious nature of the process indicates the limited availability of supplies.

Evidence of bronze-working at Thetford was also uncovered, along with three pottery kilns; and in excavations in 1966, an 11th-century kiln yard was found, about 450 metres to the north-west. A large area of the residential quarter of the town has also been uncovered.

Thetford declined after the Norman Conquest, probably because of damaging competition with the new port at King's Lynn. The settlement itself switched to the north bank of the river, for reasons not yet understood, and by the early 12th century the area of the Saxon town was

almost deserted. By the 13th century only the churches stood out among
the ploughland, and very few of these outlasted medieval times. The site
has once more been taken up for building in our own day.

Mawgan Porth
Dark Age
Settlement
Cornwall

Between c. AD 850 and 1050 a Dark Age settlement stood at the head of
this lovely bay on the west Cornish coast, on land sloping down to a
stream which flows towards the sea. The excavated remains are of a
number of courtyard houses, independent of each other, but grouped
together to form a village or hamlet where several families would have
lived. The principal room of each house is strikingly reminiscent of the
Anglo-Saxon long-house form, adapted to local conditions, and there are
other indications that the dwellers in this remote spot belonged culturally
with Saxon England.

Today blown sand has formed high drifting dunes on the seaward side.
The incidence of this sand was the reason for the abandonment of the

Left Part of the industrial quarter of late Saxon Thetford, as it might have appeared in the 10th century AD.

Dark Age settlement, and also for the preservation of its remains. It ruined pasturage, as well as making life unendurable for the inhabitants, but the houses were vacated without haste, and very few possessions were left for the 20th-century excavators to find. The refugees—such as they were, though no act of war drove them out, for this was an age of peace in Cornwall—probably moved inland to the comparatively modern village of St Mawgan. Sherds of their distinctive bar-lip pottery have been found there, which suggests a continuity of culture.

When the site was excavated in 1950–54, not only were the building plans of the houses traced, but the method of their construction was skilfully deduced. First, it seems, the turf was removed and set aside to be used to cover the roofs. Then a layer of red clay was scraped off the underlying soft rock, and the hillside was cut away to form a level platform, the spoil being spread out downhill to enlarge it. Towards the upper edge of the platform, parts of the soft rock were left standing to form the foundations of walls; and where doorways were intended, the necessary openings were cut.

Courtyard house at Mawgan Porth, as it might have appeared in the 10th century AD, looking north-west.

The positions of the walls having been pegged out, pieces of rock and boulders were laid along them in two parallel lines, to form wall-faces. The spaces between were filled with clay and fragments of stone, and so the walls were built up to the required height—about 2.2 metres. The

interstices were plugged with yellow clay from the valley bottom. The average wall thickness was 0.76 metre. The roofs, supported by central timber uprights, with rafters resting on the wall tops, were covered with branches and finally with turves, held down with perforated weights.

Each courtyard house may be thought to have accommodated one family. In the example shown in the drawing, the 'long-house' measured 10.1 metres by 3.4 metres internally, with doors in each of its long walls, and one in the east end. Cattle were partitioned off beyond the cross passage, and the rest of the house was equipped for human habitation. Other buildings enclosing the courtyard provided further accommodation. In the foreground, to the left of the narrow entrance passage, are the remains of a building, which had been demolished or allowed to fall into decay while the other parts of the house were still in use: it may have belonged to an earlier phase of the settlement. The courtyard was drained at its south-west corner, and the rainwater was led down the hillside in a rock-cut gully, roofed over with flat stone slabs.

Behind the house, on the hillside, was the cemetery. It has not been completely excavated, and it is thought that a small church, or anchorite's cell, may yet be lying hidden in the sands.

Mawgan Porth Dark Age Settlement 2
Cornwall

In the drawing of the interior of the 'long-house', the viewpoint is from the west end, looking towards the entrance opening to the courtyard. On the right is the exterior door of the house, and the opening in the opposite wall gave access to an inner room or annexe. Archaeological evidence suggests that only a low wall divided the byre from the annexe, so that fodder could have been stored beyond it, and pitch-forked over when required.

The blown sand, which in the 11th century caused the abandonment of the settlement, had preserved many things, even superficial characteristics, in a remarkable way. That the area depicted in the foreground of the drawing was a byre, for instance, was proved by the churned-up condition of the floor. It was deeply scoured around the central post, where the cattle had pawed and fidgeted, while it was untrodden against the line of the partition, where the animals could not place their hooves because of the bulkiness of their bodies. On the other hand, the further part of the floor was flat and smooth and clearly used for human habitation.

Box-like bunks lined this eastern end of the house, with sides of slate slabs set into grooves cut in the floor: the floor level inside the bunks was slightly raised. Each was a little over 1.5 metres long and 1.1 metres wide, so that, unless the sleepers were very small, they must have lain with their knees drawn up. The bunk in the south-east corner behind the exterior door was both narrower and longer, and this may have been for the children. Bracken, straw or heather piled in the bunks would have softened the hardness of rock and slate.

The hearth was a hole scooped out of the floor. One of the central roof supports seems to have been removed to make room for it. A hole in the roof would, no doubt, have been provided to draw off the smoke, but this was perhaps an optimistic rather than a practical measure. Evidence of

Interior of long-house, as
it might have appeared
in the 10th century AD.

a metal trivet or pot-stand was found: it was clear, however, that the tools and implements of the settlers were mainly of bone and stone.

The woman in the drawing is shown holding one of this people's curious bar-lip pots, examples of which have been found at other sites in Cornwall and in eastern England. These had two raised and opposed bulges in the otherwise plain rim, and within each bulge a strap or bar of clay had been inserted. Around this internal bar the thongs of the pot would have been tied, so protecting them from the flames when the pot was suspended over the fire. This peculiar form is of North European origin, and although the Cornish examples were not imported but made locally, they were clearly inspired by North European types. The connection is most interesting, and indicates a dramatic breakaway from the Mediterranean Classical forms, whose import had until the 8th century tenuously linked Cornwall with the south. Bar-lip pottery at Mawgan Porth means that the Celtic West was becoming part of the North European culture, and that, with Saxon England, it was beginning to derive ideas and forms from a common source.

Medieval and later

Wharram Percy in the Yorkshire Wolds is the best-known and most extensively excavated deserted medieval village site in Britain. The peasant houses at Wharram were mainly of the traditional long-house type, with a byre or storage place at one end, and living quarters at the other. The houses vary considerably in size, and no great effort seems to have been made to obtain square corners or even parallel walls. The walls were generally half-timbered, resting on a few courses of chalk blocks, quarried on site. The roofs were often of the flimsiest materials, and the narrowness of the houses may be due to the poor quality of the roof timbers available to the peasant builders.

Almost every house in the village appears to have been rebuilt each generation, sometimes at right-angles to its previous alignment, sometimes encroaching upon its neighbour's ground, with a remarkable disregard for property rights. Indeed, the yard and garden boundaries of the settlement were in a constant state of flux in the medieval period. By contrast, the field system around the village continued with little change.

In Saxon times, the settlement was concentrated in the valley around the church, which in its earliest timber phase may date from the 10th century or earlier. In Domesday Book (1086) two manor houses are mentioned, and six plough teams were maintained. The village was acquired by the Percy family in the late 12th century, probably for a bastard son. At this date a new manor house was built at the top of the slope north of the church. Peasant houses also spread up from the valley ground, and when the manor house was given up, probably on the failure of the family line, they took over its site.

In the 13th century a younger, legitimate branch of the Percy family returned to Wharram, and again a manor house was built, but this time at the extreme north end of the village. More peasant houses were constructed at this period, between the site of the old manor and the new, but this time evidently according to a fixed plan, for all were laid out gable end on to the street. The little church of St Martin went through a similar process of growth and elaboration, from timber to stone, and with the addition of aisles, tower and chancel, reaching its greatest extent at the date shown in the drawing.

The village ceased to exist c. 1500, when the arable fields were all converted into sheep pastures, and the villagers were evicted. According to Sir Thomas More, the churches themselves in such villages were often converted into sheephouses, but this was not the case at Wharram: indeed, although it stood alone among the ruins, services continued to be held in the church until 1949, after which time the fabric succumbed to

Wharram Percy medieval
village from the south, as
it might have appeared
at the beginning of the
15th century.

thieves and the weather. Its ruins have now been consolidated by the
Department of the Environment, into whose hands guardianship of the
site has passed.

Rayleigh Mount
Essex

After landing, apparently unopposed, on English soil, the Norman invaders moved quickly to consolidate their position and raised a castle by
the shore. The Bayeux Tapestry records the incident: workmen are
shown throwing up earth to complete the castle mound, upon which a
timber structure has already been erected. Other examples of the motte-
castle can be seen earlier in the Tapestry, notably those at Dol and Dinan,
and these furnish us with some pictorial evidence of the castle type that
was to be the visible symbol of the Conquest in England, and which
survived in use in some places into the 14th century.

Rayleigh Mount is first recorded in Domesday Book, and was the
centre of a barony that included much land in southern Essex. The early
castle was a typical Norman motte: a natural mound heightened with
spoil thrown up from the deep ditch that was dug to isolate it at the end
of a spur of rising land. A wooden tower was erected on this spoil heap,

Rayleigh Mount, as it might have appeared in the late 13th century, viewed from the west.

defended by a palisade; and on the other side of the ditch a simple enclosure, containing the huts of soldiers and servants, lay between the castle and an existing Saxon village to the east.

This rough-and-ready arrangement continued until c. 1130–c. 1160 (the dates correspond significantly with the anarchy of Stephen's reign), and only then, it seems, were ditches dug to encircle both the mound and the enclosure completely, so creating a full motte-and-bailey castle. This was repaired and improved in the following century, while ancillary buildings in the bailey increased in importance. The evidence suggests that the castle was deserted by about 1350.

There is nothing to indicate stone building or fortification at Rayleigh, though the motte was revetted with Kentish ragstone and flint rubble, presumably to stabilise the loamy clay. However, excavation has disclosed an elaborate timber bridge and the flimsy semi-circular barbican, shown in the foreground of the drawing. Perhaps fortunately, the castle seems never to have been put to the test of war.

The asymmetric arrangement of motte-and-bailey castles, with the motte exposed on the edge of the outwork, has never been satisfactorily explained, unless we accept it as a glorified bolt-hole, not intended to withstand a serious siege. The exact appearance of the motte-tower itself remains a matter for conjecture: the rectangular markings, shown here, each with a round boss in its centre, occur on the Dol motte-tower in the Tapestry, and also on a carved capital (dated c. 1090–1100) from Westminster Hall, and now in the Victoria and Albert Museum, which depicts such a castle. It is suggested that these were rows of loopholes through which spears could have been thrust at the enemy—making the tower like 'a hedgehog with lunging bristles' (Hope-Taylor).

Bramber Castle
West Sussex

Bramber Castle was a stronghold of William de Braose, one of William the Conqueror's barons, who is known to have been granted much land in Sussex. The castle stands on a knoll of chalk, high above the River Adur, a natural defensive position that was further improved when a deep ditch was dug around the site. The Adur (it was not embanked until the 16th century) wound through a wide estuary to the east, which at high tide became a glittering expanse of sea. A channel was cut from the main stream to allow boats of shallow draught to approach the eastern ditch.

The original castle on the site was a motte, all but surrounded by a horseshoe-shaped quarry ditch, 16.8 metres in width and between 3.6 and 4.6 metres deep. This motte, and the timber tower and palisade which, it is reasonable to assume, surmounted it, was soon abandoned—perhaps because it was badly constructed and unstable—and in its decay, the quarry ditch silted up again. At an early date, therefore, the focus of the castle shifted south to the entrance gate, where a substantial gatehouse of flint and stone, measuring 11.6 by 12.5 metres externally, was built. In conjunction, a battlemented flint and stone outer curtain, complete with wall walk, was also constructed to enclose the site. Here too excavation has revealed faulty workmanship: the curtain fell down in pieces soon after its erection, and in some places was rebuilt three times—hence the scaffolding poles in the drawing.

Gatehouse tower and curtain can be dated to about 1100. The church, dedicated to St Nicholas, is contemporary with the first phase of the castle, and would seem to have presented a hazard to the defenders of the second phase, though it was separated from the gatehouse by the ditch. It is possible that the church itself was defended. Domestic buildings lined the castle wall, probably workshops on the north, and a hall and kitchen on the west. On the east side are the remains of a later structure, with a projection beyond the curtain.

At a later date, c. 1140–50, the entrance archway of the gatehouse was blocked, so that the structure could support the weight of an upper storey which was then added. This tall tower easily dominated the church and landscape, and remained the dominant feature of the castle until the 15th century, when there is evidence of general ruin and decay. The new entrance to the castle was probably made in the curtain further west.

Bramber with its gatehouse keep may be compared with the little timber castle at Penmaen in the Gower Peninsula in South Wales. This stands dramatically on a seacoast headland, and, rather like Bramber, the site has been separated from a gentle landward approach by a ditch, in this case cut from the rock. Excavation has disclosed a two-storeyed timber hall in the bailey, but, clearly, the timber gatehouse is the most important single feature. It is thought that the curtain wall in this case was of wattle, and it stood on a massive defensive bank. The gatehouse was, almost inevitably, burnt down, and one wonders why, with excellent building stone abundant at Penmaen, it should ever have been timber-built, for the land was hostile and danger must have been ever present.

Bramber Castle from the south, as it might have appeared in the early 12th century.

Totnes Castle
Devon

Judhael, a follower of William the Conqueror, was granted over 100 manors in Devonshire, and the Saxon borough of Totnes. The motte of the castle he raised there (the bulk of it is artificial), extended into the town. A square wooden tower stood on the summit, the drystone foundations of which have been traced to a depth of 3.4 metres within the motte, and possibly reached down to its base. This may have been surrounded by a wooden palisade; certainly, there was a palisade around the bailey, and a deep, steep-sided ditch, 21.3 metres wide.

Totnes exhibits the translation, common in the south and south-west, of the motte-and-wooden tower arrangement into a motte with stone walls, or shell-keep. Here the change probably occurred early in the 13th century, by which time the original wooden tower would have collapsed and decayed. The defences of both motte and bailey were then re-constructed in stone, following their original lines.

The first stone structure on the motte was thin and weak, but it was substantially restored and improved in the following century. Parts of the inner circumference of the shell—which was otherwise hollow and open—were lined with lean-to sheds. The wall walk was 4.6 metres above the courtyard, and was reached by two staircases in the thickness of the wall. The garderobe projecting beyond the shell on the west side, where it ad-joins the curtain, was a later addition, and its thin walls made an obvious weakness in the defence: its peculiar position may mask the site of the original entrance. The summit of the motte was reached by steps following the west curtain.

The stone curtain of the bailey was restored at the same time as the

Below right The 12th-century castle at Penmaen in Gower.

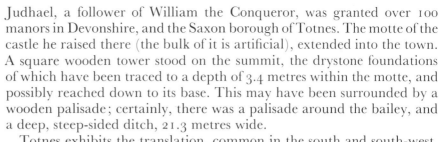

113

Totnes Castle from the north-east, as it might have appeared in the 14th century.

shell-keep, in the 14th century, and traces of domestic buildings have been found in the bailey ground.

There is evidence that, as early as 1343, the castle was permanently in the hands of stewards of the lord, and was maintained merely as a symbol of feudal tenure. This state of affairs continued through the centuries. The defences were kept in repair, while the domestic buildings fell away: at length, Totnes passed from passivity into ruin.

Rochester Castle
Kent

The existing stone tower-keep at Rochester stands within the bailey enclosure of the second castle to be built there. The first, of a motte-and-bailey type, is thought to have been erected soon after the Conquest, on Boley Hill, south of the present site—'boley' is no doubt a corruption of 'bailey'. There Odo, Bishop of Bayeux, William's half brother, was besieged in 1088, when he joined the rebellion against the young William Rufus; and when, at length, he surrendered and left the country in disgrace, the original castle was probably destroyed.

The earliest work in stone on the present site and in the cathedral can be ascribed to Gundulf, Bishop of Rochester, who also supervised the building of the White Tower at London. The decision to build the castle

Rochester Castle, from the north-west, as it might have appeared in the later Middle Ages.

apparently arose after complicated haggling between Gundulf ('very competent and skilful at building in stone'), William Rufus, and Lanfranc, Archbishop of Canterbury. The King had demanded £100 for the confirmation of certain property rights: the clerics said they had no money, and so, in lieu of payment, the King agreed to accept a castle built at Gundulf's expense. In the event, the Bishop erected the building for a mere £60.

Gundulf's castle consisted of a walled enclosure, with entrance gate and at least one mural tower, and a ditch on the landward side. The great keep was added in c. 1127, when Henry I granted the Constableship of the castle to Archbishop William de Corbeil (Archbishop of Canterbury) and his successors in office 'for ever'. Corbeil's tower, four floors high, was 34.5 metres to the top of the battlements, and the corner turrets rose a further 3.6 metres above that. The foundation walls were 3.6 metres thick. The plan, excluding the forebuilding, is almost exactly square, divided by a cross wall which contains a well shaft. The position of the keep reflects the lingering strength of the motte-and-bailey tradition.

The dangers of placing a royal castle more or less in private hands were amply demonstrated in 1215, when Archbishop Stephen Langton handed his stronghold over to the rebel barons against King John. The King lay then at Dover, and the rebels hoped, by controlling Rochester, to keep him from London, which was also in rebel hands. John, arriving at speed, at once laid siege to the castle: stone-throwing engines were brought up to pound the defences, and were augmented 'day and night' by a barrage of arrows and crossbow bolts. At the same time, the bridge across the Medway (in the bottom left-hand corner of the drawing) leading to London and safety, was cut.

At length, Gundulf's curtain was breached in the south-east corner, and the defenders retreated into the keep. Now pioneers were called in to undermine the nearest angle of the keep, and when their work was done, an urgent command was sent out by the King for 'forty of the fattest pigs of the sort least good for eating' to fill the excavated space with combustible material. Fire was applied, and in the roaring and sizzling blaze, the miners' timber props dissolved, and down tumbled an entire corner of the keep. The defenders hurriedly withdrew into the other half of the tower where, after a desperate resistance, all were captured.

In the hands of John's successors, Rochester was extensively repaired, and the damaged corner of the keep rebuilt, but this time in the form of a round turret. A wall was also erected across the bailey on the north side of the keep. Then, in 1264, the castle was besieged again, this time by supporters of Earl Simon de Montfort against the forces of King Henry III. Again the bailey was penetrated, and the keep was closely pent for a week, until news that the King himself was coming up with an army caused the rebel forces to withdraw.

After this, for 100 years, the castle fell into decay. Edward III obviously thought it of strategic importance, however, for it was restored by him between 1367 and 1370 at a cost of £2,262, and two mural towers were added to the defences of the eastern curtain. Richard II after him had the north-west bastion built (this is in the left foreground of the drawing). This ended the architectural development and, indeed, the military history of the castle, which by the 16th century had again fallen into decay.

Framlingham Castle
Suffolk

Although Framlingham is linked by legend with the martyred Saxon King Edmund, the first buildings on the site date from the reign of Henry I, who granted it to Roger Bigod, c. 1101. Normally, one would have expected some evidence of motte-and-bailey, but here there is no artificial mound, and Bigod's stronghold, set within ditch and palisade, was a fortified timber dwelling-house rather than a castle, with an outer bailey similarly defended for his retainers to the south.

Bigod's son, Hugh, first Earl of Suffolk, reconstructed the main domestic buildings in stone, but the original timber defences were left standing. It was this castle that Henry II ordered to be demolished in 1175–77, after Hugh's second unsuccessful rebellion against him, but the royal engineers seem to have been content with dismantling the wooden defences. The domestic buildings were certainly still standing, despite the order, when Hugh's son Roger proceeded to rebuild the curtain wall in stone, c. 1178–1213, for he incorporated them in his work.

Hugh's hall and solar, with its two cylindrical chimneys, and the

jutting chapel of contemporary date adjoining, appear on the right of the drawing. The chapel roof, in fact, extended under the wall walk, and the lower walls of the Chapel Tower, as can be seen, were stepped back to avoid it. It has been suggested that a decorative arcading, traces of which have been found on the inner face of this tower alone, was placed there to remind men on the wall walk that they were passing over the chapel altar.

On the opposite side of the courtyard stood the later great hall, built c. 1200 (the earlier hall was not demolished, but continued to provide additional accommodation). A wooden fence helped to seclude this end of the courtyard, with its flower garden: this was the lord's (and his lady's) private domain. The building with the central louvre (left fore-ground) was a kitchen; and there was a roofed well-house (right fore-ground) and a path leading from the main gate.

The great interest of Framlingham resides in its curtain wall and 13 massive towers, all (save one) square in plan, which survive to this day in an almost perfect state. It is claimed that the knowledge gained by the Crusaders of Byzantine fortification was applied here. It is even suggested that the walls of Constantinople were a possible prototype—

whose towers, indeed, are of almost exactly this height. Here was a new model to set against the traditional motte-and-bailey. Ten of the towers have open backs—they were boarded above the wall walk with timber-framed walls—and there was a continuous arched passage through all 13 towers, a timber bridge being thrown across the gorge in each case. (By removing the planks in times of danger, sections of the wall walk could thus be isolated.) The fighting platforms on the tops of the towers can only have been reached by ladders from the wall walk.

The retention of these early square towers at Framlingham—so vulnerable to undermining, as the siege of Rochester had shown—is evidence that the ensuing history of the castle was peaceful, and this was indeed the

case. Here Mary Tudor stayed in 1553, after the death of Edward VI, when her succession was still in doubt: her standard floated over the gatehouse tower, and her followers in increasing numbers encamped about the castle. But there was no more pageantry for Framlingham after that, and within a century, the great hall had become a poor-house.

Old Sarum Cathedral
Wiltshire

The outer earthworks of Old Sarum, a mile and a quarter north of modern Salisbury, are generally reckoned to date from the early Iron Age, and enclose an area of about 12 hectares. Here, or in the immediate vicinity, the Roman posting station of Sorviodunum was established, and its Saxon successor, Searoburh or Searesbyrig, was probably resettled on the hilltop site in the reign of King Alfred. A mint founded in the Saxon town in the time of Ethelred the Unready continued to strike silver pennies until the first coinage of Henry II.

At the Norman Conquest an earthen motte was raised in the very centre of the old enclosure, and a royal wooden castle built there, to dominate the town. Transverse banks and ditches, running north and south, linked the castle to the outer defences—which were themselves re-dug and strengthened at about this time—and neatly divided the town in two. To the east would have lain the outer bailey of the castle and the main gate: in the area to the west the Norman cathedral was sited.

The first cathedral on the site was begun in 1078 and completed in 1092, under Bishop St Osmund. It was 52.7 metres long from east to west, with an apsidal east end (terminating under the crossing of the later church); and 34.6 metres wide across the transepts, which were equipped with towers, as at Exeter Cathedral. Five days after its consecration, this great church was almost completely demolished in a storm, only the nave surviving.

Osmund's successor, Bishop Roger, commenced the rebuilding on an even grander scale. He took as his model the Abbaye-aux-Dames at Caen in Normandy, and created the church that is shown in the drawing, adding twin turrets and an imposing facade at the west end; a great central tower; transepts aisled on both east and west sides (with an entrance porch on the south transept); and a much-extended quire and presbytery to the east, with three apsidal eastern chapels (squared externally). A cloister was also placed on the north-east. The final dimensions of the cathedral were: 96.3 metres from end to end, and 42.1 metres across the transepts. The richness of the work is attested by numerous architectural fragments recovered in the course of excavations.

While this magnificent work was proceeding, Bishop Roger sought and obtained the King's permission to rebuild the royal castle, practically converting it into a bishop's palace, where he appears to have lived in some state. Then, involving himself in the civil wars between Stephen and Matilda, he fell from grace, and died in 1139. His estates were seized, the castle was re-occupied and much fortified by the King, and a chillier regime followed, with mutual suspicions between priests and soldiery.

The troubles came to a head in 1217 when the dean and clergy, re-

Old Sarum Cathedral from the south-east, as it probably appeared about 1130.

turning from a Rogationtide procession to one of the new churches established beyond the town, found the great east gate of the outer bailey barred against them, and were told that the garrison feared an attack from the Germans! The indignant clergy retaliated by petitioning Pope and King for the removal of the cathedral to the valley below, adding a store of related grievances: the incivility of the soldiers; the exorbitant rents charged for the accommodation of the poor clerks (again by the military); the scarcity of water; the constant exposure to high winds that almost drowned the voice of the officiating priest; the ruinous condition of the fabric; and so on. Most potent of all must have been the gradual depopulation of the hilltop town, which, as early as 1183, was already being described as 'Old Salisbury'.

The clergy's petition was accepted, and the foundations of the new Salisbury Cathedral were laid on 8 April 1220. In 1331 the dean and chapter were licensed to remove stones and mortar from the walls of the old church for the repair of the new, and they made a thorough job of it. Old Sarum Cathedral, buried under the grass, was lost until 1834, when a severe drought caused the old foundations to be discovered. Measurements were then taken, and intermittent excavation commenced.

Castle Acre Priory
Norfolk

The Cluniac Order was introduced into England by William de Warenne, first Earl of Surrey, a follower of William the Conqueror. Three monks from the Abbey of Cluny in Burgundy (to which all Cluniac daughter-houses were subordinate) were settled at a priory at Lewes in Sussex, and from there the Order spread rapidly through the country.

Castle Acre Priory in Norfolk was almost certainly founded by William's son, the second earl, and is one of the best-preserved Cluniac houses in England. Originally settled in the outer bailey of the castle, east of Castle Acre village, the community removed at an early date to a more convenient spot on low ground to the south-west, for buildings were in construction here by the year 1090. The whole of the church, up to and including the choir, belongs to this early period, as do the lower storeys of the towers flanking the west front. The presence of pointed arches in the upper storeys, however, indicates that the work here continued into late Norman times. The great Perpendicular window was inserted over the door in the 15th century, partly destroying three tiers of Norman arcading, an alteration that can be paralleled in the west fronts of Rochester and Durham Cathedrals. Nor would the church have been less proudly decked within: hung, as it must have been, with paintings; adorned with jewelled crosses and copious ornament; and with the vestments of the monks in keeping with such splendour.

All the buildings of the cloister—placed, as was usual, on the south side of the church, to catch the sun—were added in the mid-12th century. They were: the chapter house and additional small rooms on the east side, with the monks' dormitory over; the *frater* or refectory on the south; and the *cellarium* or store-house on the west, with guest hall and prior's lodging over. Less orthodox are the buildings that occupy the foreground of the drawing, obscuring the western range. These were all late 15th-

3 Lullingstone Roman villa from the south, as it might have appeared in about AD 360.

4 Tintern Abbey from the west, as it might have appeared in the early 16th century.

and early 16th-century encrustations. Most prominent is the prior's chapel and solar, with its fine bow window, placed at right angles to the west front of the church. The steeply pitched roofs behind cover later second-storey additions to the prior's lodging (with chimney) and to the original porch, perhaps to provide more guest rooms. A new porch with low roof was extended to the west. The staircase giving direct access to the guest hall from the outer court was of 14th-century date.

On the right of the drawing, the small building with smoking chimney was the detached 15th-century kitchen, built over the stream. The same stream, further down, flowed under the rere-dorter (latrine block) at the end of the dormitory, past the infirmary with its tall chimneys, and away into the distance under the precinct wall.

On the left of the drawing, the low building adjoining the north transept was the sacristy, where the sacred vessels and vestments were kept. In the field behind, scattered crosses mark the monks' cemetery.

Discipline appears to have been none too strict in the Cluniac houses of the English province. Great wealth encouraged the abuses that the Order had arisen to eradicate; indeed, the domestic history of Castle Acre has been described as a succession of more or less serious scandals. Also, in later days the priory seems to have operated with less than a full complement, for in 1537, when it was surrendered to Henry VIII, only the prior and ten monks signed the deed.

Byland Abbey
North Yorkshire

The Cluniac revival, for all its splendour, was spiritually short-lived. The Cistercian Order, which arose towards the end of the 11th century from the Abbey of Cîteaux on the borders of Burgundy and Champagne, had a longer and more honourable existence. Alerted to the temptations that had beset their predecessors when they established themselves near the seats of worldly power, the Cistercians sited their own monasteries, by choice, in wild and remote places, difficult of access. And whereas both Cluniac and Benedictine monks adorned their churches, for the greater glory of God, the Cistercians were all for plainness and simplicity. Their vestments were to be plain and unembroidered, their crosses of painted wood, the chandeliers of iron, the censers of copper or iron, the church plate of silver gilt. 'And let there be no stone towers for bells, nor yet wooden ones of inordinate height, such as to disgrace the simplicity of the Order'.

Sometime before 1177, after early setbacks, the Cistercians at Byland decided on the present site, then overgrown and marshy and deliberately far-removed, and 'began manfully to root out the woods, and by long and wide ditches to draw off the abundance of water from the marshes; and when dry land appeared they prepared for themselves an ample, fitting

Byland Abbey from the west, as it might have appeared in the early 16th century.

122

and worthy site'. With equal vigour, they also began exploiting the surrounding country for arable and sheep farming, for they were fine agriculturists.

The proportions of the church at Byland must have been impressive, for it was 100.6 metres long and 42.7 metres across the transepts. It was severely plain, except for the west front, with its great wheel window (7.9 metres across) and wall arcade with Early English lancets. The remainder of the church windows were round-headed. The porch with its lean-to roof was called a Galilee, and was a characteristic Cistercian feature.

The lay brothers or 'conversi' in Cistercian monasteries were always accommodated in the range on the west of the cloister—at Byland, in a building 83.8 metres long, sustained by 14th-century flying buttresses. This range is the oldest work in the monastery, which must indicate that the lay brothers were here in advance of the monks, no doubt to superintend the layout of the buildings. These lay brothers took their places in the body of the church, while the monks sang in the choir. They managed the monastery estates, and performed all worldly tasks and trades associated therewith, leaving the monks free for their devotional duties. Their separate dormitory and frater would have been contained in this range, and perhaps also a separate infirmary.

Here, as in all Cistercian houses, the lay brothers lived in the monastery, instead of upon outlying farms, and this restricted the space available around the cloister. To ease the constriction, the monks' frater on the south side of the cloister (seen here behind the smoking cowl of the monastic kitchen) was commonly set at right-angles, instead of parallel to it, as in the houses of the other Orders. The warming house with its chimney would also have been on this side: this was the only room, apart from the kitchens and infirmary, where a fire was allowed. Chapter house, below, and monks' dormitory, above, were in their normal position, adjoining the south transept of the church.

The low building enclosing the additional small courtyard to the right was the lay brothers' rere-dorter. Immediately beyond this, the clustered chimneys of the meat kitchen can be seen, where meat dishes were prepared for guests and the sick. The separate block in the distance was the infirmary.

At its suppression in 1539, Byland had 25 monks and an abbot, and the annual income was £295.

Rievaulx Abbey	Rievaulx Abbey in Yorkshire was the earliest Cistercian house in the

**Rievaulx Abbey
The Frater**
North Yorkshire

Rievaulx Abbey in Yorkshire was the earliest Cistercian house in the north, predating its near neighbour at Byland by 17 years. It was founded in 1131 on a somewhat constricted site, in a narrow rugged valley, a 'place of horror and waste solitude', as one monkish chronicler described it.

The church and principal buildings around the cloister were soon under construction and were more or less complete by the last quarter of the 12th century. At that time, the frater lay east-west, parallel with the church. Then, in about 1200, for the same reasons as those noted above at Byland (to provide accommodation for the lay brothers), a costly re-

Rievaulx Abbey: the
Frater, as it might have
appeared about 1320.

construction of the south side of the cloister was undertaken. The monastic
kitchen was drawn out of the western range, the frater was turned round
to stand end-on to the cloister, and the warming house was attached to its
flank on the eastern side, having been moved from its normal position
next to the chapter house. The final arrangement was very similar to that
at Byland, and, indeed, at Fountains.

In the drawing, we are looking down the frater from the door at the
cloister end. It is a fine room, 37.8 metres long by 11.6 metres wide, built
over a vaulted basement of cellars and storerooms. A seven-sided rafter
roof is shown; in the 15th century this was taken down, and one of low
pitch substituted.

The general effect must have been of austere simplicity, tempered by
the delicacy of the wall arcading and the refined proportions of the
arches on their thin supports, which were probably of coloured marble.
The glass in the windows was geometrically disposed; the floor was of
chequered tiles; and the walls, in common with the other monastic buildings, would have been given a coat of hard lime, with false joint-lines
picked out in red.

Two meals were served each day in the frater: after the services of sext and vespers (that is, at about 12.30 and 6.30) in summer, and after nones (at about 2.30) in the winter, when there was no evening meal except a drink of water. The principal meal for each monk consisted of a pound of bread and two courses of vegetables cooked without grease. Supper consisted of the remains of the pound of bread with some raw fruit or vegetables. Jugs of water or watered beer were also provided.

Regulations for eating were very strict and precise: cups to be held in both hands; arms not to be rested on the table; knives to be wiped on the bread and then cleaned on the napkin after use; no talking allowed. Each place was laid with a spoon, cup and napkin, each monk bringing his own knife, and stopping in the cloister beforehand, to wash his hands in the lead-lined water troughs set on either side of the frater door.

The abbot would not have been present—he took his meals in the guest house—and so the prior, his next in rank, presided. Service began with him in the centre of the high table, and proceeded clockwise along the right-hand side of the room; then it proceeded anti-clockwise along the left-hand side of the room, starting with the monk sitting on the prior's right hand.

Supervision of the eating arrangements was the responsibility of the cellarer, the kitchener, and two hebdomarii, or monks on kitchen duty. One of the latter approaches the foreground of the drawing. He has exchanged his white, outer tunic for the black scapular—a garment of shoulder width, bound at the sides with leather thongs—and with a black cowl, which all Cistercian monks wore for manual work.

The door on the right led out to the kitchen, and that beneath the pulpit gave access to the vaults below. The pulpit was reached by a flight of steps in the wall. Here the reader of the day would stand, reading passages of Scripture, and glancing from time to time towards the high table, to catch any correction that the prior might make. He took his meal later with the servers.

Grace was sung before dinner, and again afterwards, beginning in the refectory, but ending in the church, the monks walking there in procession, chanting the 51st Psalm.

Tintern Abbey
Gwent
(*colour plate 4*)

Tintern Abbey was founded in 1131, in the same year as Rievaulx. Here again the Cistercians chose a narrow valley site, which must have seemed wild and remote enough in the 12th century. Even six and a half centuries later, its 'steep woods and lofty cliffs' and the wild secluded scene impressed one distinguished tourist with 'thoughts of more deep seclusion', and the situation is still beautiful, even retired, today—though some of that quality is dissipated by the main Chepstow–Monmouth road, which cuts through the sites of the small buildings shown in the foreground of the drawing.

The abbey exhibits some unusual features. A Galilee porch is noticeably absent. More important, for reasons of drainage, the cloister has been placed on the north side of the church, in its shadow. The lay brothers' range, still on the west side of the cloister, does not abut against the church as normal, but is set some 12 metres back, and a small courtyard interposed, perhaps with the idea of letting more light into the cloister.

The original abbey was small in scale. Rebuilding began about 1220, with the familiar realignment of the frater and associated buildings, so that the visible remains are largely of 13th-century date.

The west front of the church contained a seven-light window; the one above it lighted the roof space above the vaulted nave. Another great window of eight lights occupied nearly the whole wall at the east end. Both set-pieces would have contained stained glass by this date. By contrast, the pointed windows above the aisle roofs were characteristically modest, and the whole building is solid and restrained, with its low tower for bells, and unusual stepped and gabled buttresses.

In the small courtyard the lay brothers' night stair can be seen, leading up from a door in the north-west angle of the church to their dormitory on the second floor of the western range. Their frater would have been on the floor below. The abbey's main entrance porch is to the left of the courtyard in this range; it led into the outer parlour (Old French *parloir*), where the monks could converse with visitors. (The upper rooms of this low building were the cellarer's lodgings.) Although vows of silence were not taken, unnecessary talk was discouraged, and would normally have been confined within the cloister to words exchanged in the inner parlour, a narrow passage room which usually adjoined the chapter house.

Behind the western range the parallel roof of the monks' frater can be seen, and the front end of the warming house beside it. The monks' dorter, with chapter house below, closed the cloister on the eastern side. The infirmary, abbot's hall and other buildings are lost behind the great bulk of the church.

In the foreground, on the extreme left, is the fishpond. The gatehouse chapel is on the extreme right: parts of this still survive, incorporated into a house. The gatehouse itself is not visible, but part of the precinct wall can be seen, enclosing 11 hectares of the abbey grounds. The great drain, roofed with stone slabs, enters the picture in the centre foreground, its water taken from a small stream further west, a tributary of the Wye. It divided to drive the abbey mill, then turned north and east under the western range. It flushed the lay brothers' rere-dorter, then that of the monks, 30.5 metres to the east; divided again to serve the infirmary, and eventually emptied into the Wye downstream. It was a complicated arrangement, and deserves the attention of those who decry the Middle Ages as a period of picturesque squalor.

Tintern Abbey, with an annual income of £192, was one of the smaller monasteries suppressed by Act of Parliament in 1535. In 1537 the site was granted to the Earl of Worcester, the abbey's patron at the time of the suppression. He stripped the lead from the roofs and melted down the bells, and left a noble ruin.

Fountains Abbey
North Yorkshire

Fountains Abbey was founded by twelve monks and the prior of the Benedictine Abbey at York who, in 1132, in protest against the laxity of that house, removed to Ripon, meaning to set up by themselves, re-formed according to the Cistercian rule. The Archbishop of York interfered, and took them under his care, and granted them land—the present

Fountains Abbey from the south-west, as it might have appeared early in the 16th century.

site—in Skelldale, in the hills to the west.

The place was suitably grim, for it was 'thick set with thorns, lying between the slopes of mountains and among rocks jutting out on both sides; fit rather, it seemed, to be the lair of wild beasts than the home of human beings'. However, there was plenty of good building stone to hand, which was quarried in the immediate vicinity.

The building of Fountains fell into three main periods. In the first, we have to imagine a typical long church, with massive Norman piers in the nave; with three round-headed windows and a rose in the west front; a low tower over the crossing; and a very short eastern arm—an entirely orthodox product of the Cistercian Order. Slightly later, the claustral buildings were erected. The western range, which is 92.1 metres long and 12.7 metres wide (12.2 metres longer than Ripon Cathedral), was built in two stages, the point of transition in styles being marked approximately by the porch on its west side. The rere-dorter of this range lies over the stream, and connects with the lay brothers' infirmary, a basilican building completely supported on four tunnels over the stream. The small building in the foreground of the drawing is believed to have been the infirmary kitchen.

The second period marks a time of great expansion in the life of the abbey. There are even signs of problems caused by overcrowding. The monks' dormitory (seen here with a double line of dormer windows) seems to have been provided with two storeys. Its roof line cuts across two windows where it abuts against the south transept, suggesting a later addition. At the end of the lay brothers' range an awkwardly placed building (seen gable end on, on the right of the drawing) would seem to indicate an addition here also, probably to provide more dormitory space. At the same time, the choir and presbytery of the church were extended eastwards, culminating in a new eastern transept, containing the famous Chapel of the Nine Altars. The other buildings that belong to this period are the monks' infirmary block (in the background of the drawing) —an enormous hall, 51.8 metres long and 21.3 metres wide, with its own chapel, kitchens and cellars—and two charming guest houses (in the foreground). These works were probably completed by the middle of the 13th century, and Fountains was then at the height of its glory and power.

For 230 years little more was done and then, towards the close of the abbey's life, a period of adornment began, indicating a relaxation of the Cistercian rule. John Darnton, abbot from 1479 to 1494, removed the original lights in the west front of the church, and those in the eastern transept also, and replaced them with great Perpendicular windows, filled with stained glass. He also attempted to heighten the central tower. The foundations, however, would not take the strain, and an ugly crack opened. A crude buttress was hastily thrown up, the crack was filled, and the work abandoned. Nevertheless, a grand tower there was to be, and since the old one was not equal to the demands made upon it, Darnton's successor, Marmaduke Huby, abbot from 1494 to 1526, proceeded to erect a new one beside it, against the north transept. This was 51.8 metres high, in four storeys, and battlemented, with twin buttresses at each corner; and eight bells were hanging in it at the time of the Dissolution, six more than were permitted by the rules of the Order! It is interesting to note, as a further indication of a changing spirit, that both men signed and dated their work: Darnton with a rebus, and Huby with his initials MH, set in an elaborate panel of stone.

The abbot, prior and thirty monks surrendered the abbey to the King in November 1539. Its annual income was then estimated at about £1,000 and assets included 1,976 horned cattle, 1,146 sheep, 86 horses and 79 swine.

Dryburgh Abbey
Borders

Dryburgh Abbey, founded in 1150, was the first of five houses of the Premonstratensians or White Canons in Scotland. This was a reformed body of Augustinian Canons, modelled by their founder, St Norbert, on the Cistercian Order, and the inmates were priests living more strictly according to the monastic rule. Like the Cistercians, the White Canons favoured retired ground for their houses, and the arrangement of the monastic buildings around the cloister conforms to the Cistercian pattern, with modifications.

Dryburgh Abbey from the south-west as it probably was in the late 15th century.

Dryburgh lies in a loop of the River Tweed, 8 kilometres south-east of Melrose. The abbey occupies a sloping site, which accounts for the three building levels. In the drawing, the concentrated main buildings are seen from the south-west. The Tweed is on the extreme right, and the deep open channel falling into it contained river water diverted across the loop from upstream, to serve and drain the domestic buildings. On the extreme left is the precinct wall with scattered houses—the abbot's lodging, the barn, bakehouse—none of which are now visible. The church, like the rest of the buildings, was constructed of warm-coloured local stone, and except for the west front (with its heavily moulded door and large pointed window, both of the 15th century), was of the late 12th and 13th centuries.

The whole of the eastern range belongs to the first period of building, in the late 12th century, and is three storeys high—which is unusual. The great window in the south transept has a stepped sill to accommodate the high roof rising against it. The ground-floor rooms in this range were the library and vestry, the parlour, the lofty chapter house with a pinnacled termination to the east, the warming house, and then—at a lower level, and separated by a passage from the foregoing apartments—the novices' day room, with the rere-dorter straddling the ditch. The dormitory of the canons and novices occupied the entire first floor between the church and novices' day room, and was connected with the church by a night-stair. The third floor, lit by dormer windows, gave additional accommodation.

The frater, with vaulted cellars below, was on the south side of the cloister. The small building in the foreground, with smoking chimney, was the kitchen. There were no lay brothers and consequently no western range: this side of the cloister was closed by a plain high wall. The gate-house and covered bridge across the water channel were a late 15th-century addition. The infirmary buildings are shown behind the rere-dorter.

Dryburgh was set in a countryside which is still well-wooded and of great beauty, but which sadly was frequently disputed, and lay in the route of invading armies, causing the abbey to be savaged on several occasions. In 1322 it was burned by the retreating forces of Edward II, enraged, it is said, at hearing the bells ringing out in celebration of their discomfiture. Again, when Richard II raided Scotland in 1385, Dryburgh was ravaged and burned, along with the monasteries of Melrose and Newbattle. Hence the 15th-century rebuilding at the western end of the church. Finally, in 1544, a large English raiding party burned and spoiled the abbey so thoroughly that it was never rebuilt.

Still the canons continued to live here, and throughout the 16th century had to suffer the attentions of successive royal commendators—lay overseers—who sapped the abbey's income for their own purposes. By 1600 the last of the canons had died, but the office of the commendator survived well into the 17th century.

Through all this time the canons had shown patient determination, dealing with endless misfortunes; and they had also quarrelled vigorously with their neighbours over land rights, in lawsuits and feuds. One of these was with the Haliburtons, ancestors of Sir Walter Scott; now Sir Walter's body lies in the ruined north transept, and this particular feud may perhaps be considered to have ended.

Earl Haig, a descendant of Petrus de Haga, an early benefactor of the abbey, also lies nearby in the burial vault of the Haigs of Bemersyde.

Jedburgh Abbey
Borders

Jedburgh Abbey is today a formidable ruin. Lacking the charm of Dryburgh or the expansive urbanity of Melrose, it suggests the closely knit strength of a fortress, rather than the more human qualities of a monastic institution. The ruins stand on the steeply sloping river bank, where the swift-flowing Jed Water turns sharply eastward before resuming its northern course to join the River Teviot. There is now a fine 16th-century bridge spanning the Jed Water: in the drawing, an earlier timber structure is shown on this site.

The abbey was a foundation of Augustinian Canons who had travelled from the Abbey of St Quentin near Beauvais in France. The church was built from 1140 onwards and was completed by the middle of the 13th

Jedburgh Abbey from the south, as it might have appeared in the late 14th century.

century, though there were some 15th-century reconstructions. Originally, it may have had an apsidal east end, but this was altered to the typical square plan at an early date. This is transitional work, with pointed windows, while the interior arcading of nave and aisles is round-arched Romanesque with a lower range of pointed arches—an instance of the confusingly indiscriminate use of round and pointed arches in Scottish medieval architecture. The 15th-century south transept, the parlour adjoining, the square chapter house, the treasury, and finally what may have been the rere-dorter over the mill-lade, enclose the east side of the cloister and project beyond it.

The dorter was on the upper floor of this east range, and the large chimney perhaps relates to the warming house. These apartments were all stepped down the steep bank, as at Dryburgh, and this has the effect of magnifying the height and grandeur of the church. The frater enclosed the south side of the cloister, with the kitchen (indicated by the chimney) and the buttery and cellars in the undercroft. Parallel to the frater on the south side was the heavily buttressed infirmary with its vaulted under-croft. The entrance archway to its left led to the kitchen and there was also a stairway leading up to the cloister. The building with the stepped gable end may have been the meat kitchen. The remaining apartments in the western range, completing the cloister enclosure, were a range of cellars below, with a kitchen serving the guest house above. In the distance, the precinct gateway can be seen, and closer at hand, the abbot's lodging.

Jedburgh Abbey, in spite of its sad history of destruction (it was wrecked and plundered in 1297, and ravaged in 1410, 1416, 1464, 1523, 1544 and 1545), or perhaps because of it, was altered, reconstructed and enlarged with remarkable energy and pertinacity. The cloister, for instance, was extended southward and westward in the 14th century, entailing a complicated partial rebuilding of the frater. It is therefore not surprising that the character of Jedburgh, borne out by what evidence remains, is one of masculine strength and vigour. The building stone is local sandstone, its colour ranging from yellow to dark red.

Fourteen years after the last destructive English assault, the abbey was suppressed at the Reformation. The cloister buildings then lay in ruins, although the church itself continued to serve the parish until 1875.

Mount Grace Priory
North Yorkshire

The Carthusian Order, founded by St Bruno at Chartreuse near Grenoble in 1084, established nine 'charter-houses' in England. Mount Grace Priory, licensed by King Richard II in 1398, was the eighth in order of date.

The Carthusian brotherhood lived not only in retirement from the world, but also, to a large extent, isolated one from another, each monk having a separate house or cell, set in a small walled garden. At Mount Grace there were seventeen cells arranged along the sides of the Cloister Garth, and a further six encroached upon the Outer Court, to the south of the church, forming a small additional cloister.

Each cell was 8.2 metres square externally and two storeys high, entered by a door in the cloister wall. The internal arrangements were identical in each case. The ground floor of the cell would have been divided by wooden partitions into four rooms: an entrance lobby, a living room with fireplace, a bedroom which also served as an oratory, and a small study. The walls, which show no sign of whitewash or plastering, must have been wainscoted. A winding stair led up into a single large room above, which would have been used as a workshop.

From the living-room door at the rear, a covered walk gave access to a stone garderobe projecting from the priory wall over the main drain. This was supplied with constantly running water from the two well-houses which stood outside and at each end of the eastern precinct wall. Pure fresh water, for domestic purposes, was piped to each cell from the octagonal stone conduit in the centre of the Cloister Garth.

In strict isolation and silence, the monks occupied themselves with reading, prayer and their labours, 'especially the writing of books'. Their daily pittance of food and drink was supplied through a hatch beside the

Mount Grace Priory, as it might have appeared from the west early in the 16th century.

outer door, with a cunningly devised right-angled turn in the thickness of the wall, so that server and inmate could not see each other. The church bell rang to prompt the brethren to the recital of prayers, for the minor canonical hours, in their own houses. Only vespers and matins were celebrated daily in the church, and the community dined together only on feast days.

The eremitical nature of the Order is well reflected in the architecture of the Outer Court. Here were no splendid buildings. The church was plain and narrow, originally an aisleless rectangle, although three chapels were added later. In the drawing, the chapter house roof is seen against the low pinnacled tower. The prior's cell adjoined the church, and the building end-on, just below the monk's cemetery in the cloister, was the frater. More imposing were the guest house and gatehouse of the western range, with the brewhouse (with chimney), bakehouse and kitchen conveniently sited between them and the frater, to serve both. To the right of the gatehouse were probably more guest rooms, and the porter's lodge, with a granary over. The southern range, on the extreme right of the drawing, contained barns and stables.

The early history of the priory is one of disputes regarding its endowment, but the later years were comparatively uneventful. Its considerable wealth enabled it to escape Henry VIII's first Act of Dissolution in 1536, but it could not avoid the fate of the greater monasteries, and closed quietly in December 1539. The guest house, much altered, is still lived in.

The Bishop's Palace, St David's
Dyfed

The Bishop's Palace, St David's, looking west, as it might have appeared from the cathedral tower in about 1530.

Saint David founded a Celtic monastery on or near the present cathedral site in this westernmost tip of Wales in the 6th century AD. Destroyed by the Vikings, it lay desolate for seven years, but by 1081 had evidently recovered, for William I worshipped at the shrine of the saint. Inevitably, before many years had passed, all Pembroke was in Norman hands, and English bishops had supplanted Welsh at St David's, which was reorganised on non-monastic lines. The first English bishop, appointed in 1115, began to rebuild the cathedral, which was the main care of his successors through the 12th and 13th centuries.

The earliest and plainest work in the Bishop's Palace, which is divided

from the cathedral by the little River Alun, is the long range of guest rooms on the far side of the courtyard, which probably date from the 13th century. The chapel, with a small tower and octagonal spire, is late 13th-century, but the porch which led to it, from both the courtyard and the guest rooms, was not added until c. 1500.

The special feature of the palace, the arcaded parapet, can be seen on the east end of the chapel, and it continues along the wall tops of the great hall adjoining, surrounds the jutting porch at the eastern end of this, and extends around the nearer block of building, which contained a kitchen, bishop's hall, solar and private chapel. This unifying arcade, whose delicate columns are supported on corbels in the form of human heads, is surmounted by a flat polychrome decoration along most of its length, the dark squares of purple sandstone alternating with lighter freestone or white spar. Most of this is the work of Henry de Gower, Bishop from 1327 to 1347: it is contemporary with the building of the great hall, but has been applied to the surface of the nearer block, which was constructed by his immediate predecessors in office. On the larger structural units, the decoration is raised in terminal square turrets with battlemented tops. More of Gower's rich work can be seen in the cathedral: it was he who removed the small Norman lights and put in great traceried windows, and the elaborate stone *pulpitum* or screen across the nave is his.

The great hall in the palace was evidently built by Gower to entertain his guests in more state than had previously been possible, but the nearer block was retained for living accommodation and ordinary use. The two ranges were connected for service purposes by a passage running from the kitchen in the nearer block to a door in the east end of the great hall. The main entrance to the great hall was through the jutting porch in its long side wall.

The only addition of any importance to be made to the palace after Gower's reconstruction in the 14th century was the wing pointing towards the battlemented wall from the bishop's solar. This contained spacious private rooms, and may have been the work of Edward Vaughan, Bishop from 1509 to 1522, who was responsible for raising the central tower of the cathedral. The low building with the large chimney adjoining the bishop's hall was an earlier kitchen. The main gateway to the courtyard was on the right. Another gateway, reached by a wooden bridge across the river, served the kitchens and had the function of a 'back door'.

The wall of the cathedral close—about a quarter of which is shown—can be seen in the background, with Porth Gwyn (the White Gate), one of four entrances, on the extreme right. There were other ecclesiastical buildings apart from the palace and cathedral in the close, and some of these can be seen. On the right of the road from Porth Gwyn was the Archdeacon of Brecon's house, and, nearer at hand, the house of the prebendary of St Nicholas.

After the Reformation no more wealthy and distinguished pilgrims came to view the relics of St David—which were secretly walled up to save them from destruction—and both cathedral and palace declined. The cathedral was kept in repair until a revival of public interest in the 18th and 19th centuries led to its restoration, but the palace was already derelict and roofless by 1700.

Rhuddlan Castle
Clwyd

In 1277, in his first campaign against Llywelyn ap Gruffydd, the last native Prince of Wales, Edward I advanced his invasion base at Chester to Flint, and ordered the construction of a castle. By August he was at Rhuddlan, and another castle was begun. Llywelyn unexpectedly surrendered soon afterwards, but the building of castles went on at various strategic points in North Wales, and they became progressively grander as the years went by. Llywelyn's rebellion of 1282 provoked a second crushing campaign and the annexation of Wales proceeded: fortresses at Conway, Harlech, Caernarvon fastened the chain of English rule upon the Principality.

Rhuddlan was designed on the concentric plan—that is, with an inner and an outer defensive ring. The inner ring protected the domestic buildings, and with high walls and towers enabled the defenders to dominate the low outer curtain: to shoot over it against the besieger, or into it, if this outer line fell. At Rhuddlan these defences are not as well integrated as they might be: the inner and outer curtains are unequal distances apart and towards the river, where the ground is steeply sloping, the interval is no less than 61 metres. But Rhuddlan was only the second in the

Rhuddlan Castle from the south-west, as it might have appeared towards the end of the 13th century.

series of Welsh castles—which are known to have been erected under the supervision of one man, the King's master mason, James of St George—and by the time that Beaumaris was built, eighteen years later, all such imperfections had been eradicated, and the ultimate in concentric planning was achieved.

Rhuddlan was ringed on three sides by a wide moat, the outer bank defended by a palisade. The fourth side was washed by the River Clwyd, which was canalised in 1282, so that, although the castle stood 3 kilometres inland, sea-going vessels could reach it with supplies. There were posterns at either end of the river wall where ships could anchor and unload in safety.

The two land-gates of the castle had causeways across the moat. The inner ward was diamond-shaped in plan, with twin-towered gatehouses at the east and west angles, and a single round tower each to north and south. These towers were each four storeys high, and almost identical in their internal arrangements. The inner curtain wall was 10.7 metres high and 2.7 metres thick, increasing to 3.4 metres where it met the corner towers, to accommodate garderobes and staircases. The wall walk was uninterrupted. Timber buildings stood on all four sides of the enclosed courtyard: they included the King's Hall and Solar, the Queen's Hall and Solar, the kitchen and the chapel. The buildings in the outer ward were also timber-framed and included a granary, forge, stables and workshops.

A town was planned and attached to this castle (as indeed to all the Edwardian castles in Wales), with the purpose of attracting English colonists: its regular layout of streets survives to this day. It was defended by a ditch, bank and stockade, and was linked to the castle by a wooden bridge across the Castle Dingle. Edward wished to have it created a cathedral city, by transferring the see of St Asaph, 4.8 kilometres to the south, and appealed to the Pope to this end in 1281, but the plan came to nothing.

The castle defied Owen Glendower in 1400, although the town was overrun. It was held for the King in the Civil War, and subsequently made untenable.

Conway Castle
Gwynedd

Edward I reached Conway from Rhuddlan two months after the fall in January 1283 of Dolwyddelan Castle, the last Welsh stronghold in the Conway valley, and within four days labour and supplies were being organised to build a fortress to impose English government. Castle and town walls rose side by side, and within five years a labour force of skilled craftsmen, recruited from all parts of the kingdom, had more or less brought the great project to completion. The town filled with prosperous English traders, and the castle was fitted out to receive the King and Queen.

Conway has been described as 'incomparably the most magnificent of Edward I's Welsh fortresses'. It stands on a rocky outcrop on the shore of the River Conway, 2.4 kilometres from the open sea, one long side protected by the Gyffin stream, which flows into the river, and the other defending the harbour of the town. Part of the town can be seen on the left-

Conway Castle from the south-west, as it might have appeared at the time of its completion, about 1290.

hand side of the drawing, where one section of its wall adjoins the low barbican protecting the castle's landward entrance. Beyond this, a further section of town wall skirts the shore of the estuary and quayside.

The castle, dominated by eight round towers, was divided into an inner and an outer ward by an elaborately defended internal cross wall. The inner ward, which contained the royal apartments, had a tower at each corner of its quadrilateral courtyard, each tower flanked by a small round turret, no doubt designed to carry flag poles, for flying the royal standard when the King was in residence. There was a separate entrance and barbican to this ward on the eastern river side, so that the King, arriving from the sea, could enter his castle in private and perfect security. Doors could also be closed across the wall walk where inner and outer wards meet, to complete the isolation of this end of the castle.

The stone-built royal apartments occupying the south and east sides of the inner ward consisted of the King's hall, King's chamber, and presence chamber; and there was probably a timber-framed granary on the north side.

The outer ward housed the permanent garrison of the castle—the

Constable, the chaplain, a mason, a carpenter, a smith, an armourer and thirty soldiers. The Constable and his family probably occupied the two westernmost towers, which had guard houses against their inner side. The other buildings in this courtyard were the Great Hall, bowed in plan to conform to the strong outward angle of the curtain on the south side; and kitchens and stables opposite. There are traces of lime-wash still surviving on all the walls and towers of the castle, and there can be no doubt that Conway (and other fortresses of that time) were whitened externally, and must have gleamed from afar.

Very soon after the castle's completion, the conical slate or shingle roofs capping the towers proved unequal to the wet and windy Welsh climate, and lead roofs were substituted. Other necessary repairs at a later date were neglected, and the castle, at length, became uninhabitable. It was put into some kind of order and held briefly for the King in the Civil War, only to be slighted and to fall again into ruin, although the stonework to this day remains almost intact.

Harlech Castle
Gwynedd

Harlech stands on a rocky escarpment, high above the flat lands which were once the sea, with the mountains of Snowdonia to the north, some- times lit by flashing sunshine, but more often dark and sombre. Time has

Below Harlech Castle from the south, as it might have appeared at the time of its completion, about 1290.

removed the whitening from its walls, and the battlements have gone from the towers, but the fundamental structure survives little changed, the perfect simplicity of the design concealing a very high degree of art.

Harlech, begun in 1285, was built four-square, with a round tower of bold projection at each corner of an open rectangular courtyard, measuring 44.2 metres from east to west. The north and south walls converge slightly towards the west, reducing the western wall by 3.1 metres to 54.9 metres. A massive gatehouse, the equivalent of the keep in other castles, straddles the curtain on the landward side, with corner turrets facing the inner ward. This was the Constable's residence, and could be isolated from the wall walks in an emergency, and defended as an independent unit. It was reached by a causeway with two drawbridges over a wide rock-cut ditch, which also extended along the southern side of the castle.

Buildings abutted on three sides of the inner curtain: great hall, buttery and kitchen on the west wall, with tall windows overlooking the sea; chapel and bakehouse on the north; and granary and Ystumgwern Hall on the south. Ystumgwern Hall, a timber building, was transported from its original site 6 kilometres away, from the residence of Llywelyn ap Gruffydd—an unlikely, but well-authenticated proceeding. Between the chapel and bakehouse on the north wall, there was a postern leading into the middle ward, where two turrets in the low outer curtain defended a gate into the outer ward: this was balanced by a turret (but no gate) in the south outer curtain.

The wall of the outer ward enclosed the craggy hillside to north and west of the castle down to the water's edge. The southernmost section of this wall can be seen in the drawing, descending from the castle: it shielded the steep path leading up from the harbour and Watergate Tower. In addition, two platforms were sited on the hillside so that missiles from mangonels could give covering fire to parties humping supplies up the cliff. As a defensive work, the wall suffers from its excessive length, but the problem was reduced to an acceptable minimum for as long as the English fleet controlled the sea.

Harlech was almost complete by 1290. In 1294–95, a garrison of thirty-seven men successfully held it against the rebellious Welsh, during the rising of Madoc ap Llywelyn. Owen Glendower captured it in 1404 'in return for a sum of money'—not by assault—and for four years made it his capital and family home. It was besieged by the Yorkists in 1468, and twice during the Civil War, which brought its active history to an end.

Beaumaris Castle Anglesey
Gwynedd

Caernarvon, while yet building, fell to the Welsh under Madoc in 1294, who held it for six months, and overran Anglesey. The castle at Beaumaris was begun in the following year, and was deliberately sited in the trouble zone to reassert English authority. It sealed the northern end of the Menai Straits, as Caernarvon was supposed to seal the southern, and also controlled the principal ferry from Anglesey to the mainland.

Evidently, the building of Beaumaris was treated as a matter of the greatest urgency, for in 1296 the labour force amounted to 400 masons, 2,000 labourers, 30 smiths and carpenters, and 200 carters—and a strong

Beaumaris Castle from the south, begun in 1295 and left unfinished: as it might have appeared if the architect's conception had been carried to completion.

garrison was already in possession. In 1298 the castle was said to be 'complete'—that is to say, defensible, for we know that parts of the projected work were never carried out. Additions were made in later years and continued to be made into the 1320s, but the inner half of the southern gatehouse was then still unfinished, the great hall in the inner ward had not been built, and all the towers lacked their upper storeys. By 1341 the rain had got in and rotted the timbers left unprotected, and very little work was done thereafter. However, although the castle was abandoned, it was not dismantled, and much that was built in stone has survived, so that the addition in the drawing of the topmost walls and turrets is in no way an imaginative effort unsupported by positive evidence.

It is interesting to see in Beaumaris elements of the design of Harlech, which had evidently found favour as a solution of the problem of defence. Both castles are almost square in plan, with the angles strengthened by round towers; both have great gatehouses which were residential as well as defensive, and were 'strong points'; and the relationship between the inner and outer curtain walls is very similar. The siting, of course, is quite different. Beaumaris, now landlocked, stood originally on the sea shore, and was surrounded by a water-filled moat, whose level was regulated by a sluice. At high tide a fully-laden ship of forty tons could tie up in the small dock under the southern wall, protected on one flank by the pier-like projection of Gunner's Walk—which terminated in an artillery turret—and on the other by the town wall.

Land access to the castle was through the walled town and across a wooden drawbridge into the Gate next the Sea. This was asymmetrically placed to make unlicensed entry into the great south gatehouse in the inner curtain—further defended by a small barbican—the more perilous. A similar arrangement was planned for the northern gatehouse, but not completed. In this ideal concentric castle, the outer ward is completely dominated by the high inner curtain with its towers, from which a devastating fire could have been directed on any attackers below.

Symmetry is the prime quality of design at Beaumaris. The outer curtain is octagonal with no fewer than 12 mural towers. The inner ward is an almost perfect square—57.9 by 54.9 metres; the wall towers, 12.8 metres in diameter, are 18.3 metres apart, and project to within 6.1 metres of the outer curtain; and all are linked, not only by the wall walk, but also, at first-floor level, by an internal passage ventilated by shafts up to the wall walk.

The tower in the centre of the east curtain has a beautiful little chapel on its first floor, with arcaded walls and vaulted ceiling. While the castle was inhabited, the principal rooms were in the northern gatehouse. Great attention was paid to sanitation and the provision of garde-robes, which were arranged in groups on the wall walk (the small oblong shapes are their roofs and entrances).

Beaumaris was the last of Edward's castles in Wales. Begun so vigorously in 1295, unfinished at the death of Master James of St George in 1309, and never completed, it stands alone in unrealised perfection.

Criccieth Castle
Gwynedd

Edward I did not disdain to make use of and develop the Welsh fortresses captured in his campaigns, and Criccieth is one of these. It stands on the sea coast, 10 kilometres north-west of Harlech, on the opposite side of Tremadoc Bay. Not only are these two castles in sight of each other, but the date and style of the inserted English work at Criccieth strongly suggest that the building of the one, and modifications to the other, were co-ordinated and proceeded simultaneously. However, only £353 was spent on Criccieth between 1285 and 1292, as compared with more than £8,000 on Harlech over the same period, and this is a useful yardstick by which to measure the relative importance of these fortresses.

The original Welsh castle at Criccieth consisted of an enclosure roughly triangular in shape, with two or perhaps three straight-sided towers (to left and right in the drawing, and in the foreground). It was apparently built during the reign of Llywelyn the Great (the grandfather of Llywelyn ap Gruffydd), who was Prince of North Wales from 1200 until 1240. The irregularity of the curtain, the steep and narrow hilltop site, and the variable projection of the towers, are all characteristic of native Welsh work. The main residential quarters would have been in the tower on the right of the drawing, which was easily the largest of the three. The entrance gate to the castle enclosure was on the south side, further round

Criccieth Castle from the north, as it might have appeared early in the 14th century.

than Leyburn Tower on the left of the drawing, and was reached by a perilously exposed path winding along the cliff-edge—this part of the hill has now fallen or been quarried away.

Criccieth passed into the hands of the English in 1283. The English builders, reconsidering its defensive capabilities, greatly strengthened the landward approach by planting a twin-towered inner gatehouse in the northern end of the enclosure. This, somewhat awkwardly, formed the entrance to a new inner ward, lozenge-shaped in plan, which was inserted into the old work. Inner and outer curtain walls ran parallel for 16.7 metres on the north-west side of the castle, leaving a passageway 2.1 metres wide between (covered by the tiled pent roof in the drawing) which circuitously gave access to the inner ward from the south gate. After this straight length, the new inner curtain turned sharply south, to link up with Leyburn Tower, which was rebuilt from its foundations.

Various timber-framed buildings would have stood in the inner ward: those mentioned in accounts include the King's Hall and kitchen. A plumber's shop, smithy, bakehouse and stables are also mentioned, but these are more likely to have been sited in the outer ward. The castle chapel, porter's lodge and additional living quarters were contained in the inner gatehouse.

The tower in the foreground of the drawing is named in a survey of 1343 as 'Le Gynnetour' or the Engine Tower. It not only defended two sides of the outer curtain but, during the English occupation, mounted a heavy mangonel which could have directed a plunging fire upon the beach far below, to cover the landing of supplies.

Various repairs were made to the castle in the early 14th century, including the heightening of the inner gatehouse towers, and the evidence of this work is still visible. In 1404, in the same year as Harlech, Criccieth fell to Owen Glendower, who ordered it to be razed by fire. It was never afterwards inhabited or restored.

Castell–y–Bere
Gwynedd

Castell-y-Bere, 11 kilometres inland from Towyn in a fertile valley, is, like Criccieth, a castle of Welsh origin and predominantly Welsh construction. This is probably the stronghold which Llywelyn the Great, according to a Welsh chronicle, 'began to build for himself' in 1221. It

consists of a courtyard of irregular shape, with towers at or near the angles, and a fourth D-shaped tower to the south, commanding the approach. This southernmost tower was the castle strongpoint, containing the private apartments of the prince, and was isolated from the rest of the castle, during the Welsh occupation, by a rock-cut ditch.

At the northern extremity of the courtyard stood another elongated D-shaped tower of similar proportions, with an exterior stair to the first floor. This is believed to have housed the castle chapel, which was decorated with fine stone carving. More sculptured stone, of a high standard of craftsmanship, was found in association with the round tower dominating the barbican, and also in the inner gatehouse. The pieces recovered include fragmentary figures of foot-soldiers carrying lances, which probably flanked a doorway, and ornate foliage capitals.

The courtyard contained a smithy, and other less certain structures—and also a well, which was cleared in 1951 and found to contain the staves of several oaken buckets, one complete enough to permit restoration.

Edward I ordered the capture of the castle in April 1283, and it fell after a siege, on the 25th of that month. An English garrison was installed, a borough created, and 5 masons and 5 carpenters remained behind to carry out various works. A total of just over £262—a comparatively small amount—was expended on repairs and improvements between 1286 and 1290. The one substantial piece of building undertaken appears to have been the construction of two short sections of curtain wall linking the isolated south tower with the rest of the castle, and enclosing a previously open area.

During Madoc's rebellion in 1294, the castle was besieged by the Welsh, and Edward dispatched an expedition to relieve it, declaring that 'its safety we desire with all our heart'. It is not known what happened next, but it is to be presumed that the castle was overrun and then abandoned, for it makes no further appearance in the royal accounts, and there is evidence of destruction by fire.

Castell-y-Bere, as it might have appeared at the end of the 13th century.

Kidwelly Castle
Dyfed

Rather earlier than the Edwardian castles, was Kidwelly, situated on the west bank of the River Gwendraeth, at the head of a navigable estuary, one of many Norman foundations in South Wales. It commanded the main road to the west, which crossed the river at this point and passed between the two gateways of the walled town.

The site was granted to Bishop Roger, the builder of Old Sarum Cathedral, in 1106. All that survives of his castle is the semi-circular ditch enclosing the later towers on all sides but the east, where the steep fall to the river afforded natural protection.

In about 1275 the inner ward—an open rectangle with a round tower at each angle—was rebuilt in stone. The entrances to this were simple and weak, and a semi-circular earthen rampart, following the inner line of the ditch, probably still enclosed and defended the whole. This was replaced by the stone outer curtain in the early 14th century, and strengthened with four half-round towers, with gatehouses to north and south. Kidwelly had become a concentric castle, albeit of a somewhat unusual type.

The southern gatehouse can be seen in the drawing, and it was by far the larger of the two, an elaborate and powerful structure, complete with

Kidwelly Castle, from the south, as it might have appeared in 1500.

its own hall, solar, kitchen and smaller rooms. As at Harlech, it could be isolated as a refuge and independent defensive point. Unlike Harlech's gatehouse, it stood on the line of the outer rather than the inner curtain, a position determined for it by the pre-existing layout of the site.

When the building of the outer curtain and gatehouses was complete, the four towers of the inner ward lost their original commanding significance, and so each was heightened by the addition of another storey. The extension jutting towards the river from the south-east tower was the chapel, strengthened with massive masonry spurs. The rectangular bay on its south side was the vaulted sacristy, with the priest's room on the floor below.

The buildings occupying the inner ward of the castle were hall, solar and kitchen, with the principal rooms, as usual, on the first floor. In early Tudor times another hall was built free-standing in the confined space of the outer ward, and there were other buildings here by this date, including a bakehouse near the north gatehouse.

The town wall was probably built in the early 14th century. Its main south gateway is still in a relatively good state of preservation. The castle mill was outside the wall, fed by a mill leat diverted from the river above the weir to the east of the castle.

The town ditch, but not its wall, extended northward, curving round to link up with the riverside scarp, and may have enclosed a drill ground. It is odd that, with extravagant care lavished on the south side of the castle, this north side should have been comparatively neglected, especially as this was the quarter from which attack would surely have come. However, it never did come; Kidwelly played a merely passive role in the throttling of free Wales, and became uninhabitable at a comparatively early date.

Goodrich Castle
Herefordshire

The castle is perched on a rocky promontory, commanding a crossing of the River Wye, 5 kilometres south of Ross. It is naturally defended by steep falls to the river on the north and west, and a deep and wide moat has been carved out of the red sandstone to isolate it on the east and south.

There was a castle here before the end of the 11th century, when the Normans captured and occupied the border region west of the river— 'Goodrich' derives from 'Godric', the name of the original builder, though no fragment of his work survives. The small Norman keep dates from the mid-12th century, when the outer defences would probably have been of earth and timber. These were later built up in stone as a square enclosing wall with angle towers, only to be almost entirely rebuilt in their present form at the end of the 13th century. The barbican and an outer ward on the north and west sides were added soon after—one of the low corner turrets of the outer curtain is just visible on the extreme left of the drawing.

The date of the rebuilding is of interest, because parts of the castle then constructed bear a strong family likeness to the slightly earlier Edwardian fortresses in Wales, as though the architect had seen Harlech or Rhuddlan or Kidwelly and had come back to Goodrich determined to incorporate in his castle some of the elements of design he had admired there. Thus, one flank of the gatehouse, the so-called Chapel Tower, closely resembles Harlech, even to the rear staircase turret (topped by a standard in the drawing), but, because of the steeply sloping site, only half of the twin-towered complex at Harlech could be included: the result is adequate and ingenious, but asymmetrical, a quality unthinkable in the royal fortress.

The great masonry spurs on the corner towers are a reminder of similar elements at Kidwelly (in this case, Goodrich may have inspired Kidwelly). These spurs which at ground level become square platforms for the round towers, give the castle, finally, a character of its own, but, as they are founded on rock, one feels that their true military function—to make the work of attacking sappers more difficult—has been missed, and that they have been used rather as an attractive and decorative form. The beak-like projection in the south curtain is remarkable, giving additional strength to this wall. The three-tiered buttress-like form next to the south-east corner tower contained the latrines.

The barbican was a semi-circular bastion defended by an extension of the rock-cut moat, and had a towered gate with drawbridge and port-

147

cullis. The entrance on its south side was at right angles to the entrance to
the castle itself, which could only be reached over a fixed bridge with a
further drawbridge at the main gate: the defensive strength of this arrangement can be well imagined. Inside, the courtyard was enclosed on
all sides with buildings lining the curtain wall. A kitchen adjoined the
keep; the great hall and the lord's private chapel were against the west
wall; and the solar stood to the north. The outer ward was kept free of
buildings except on the west side, where stables were added in the 14th
century.

There is no siege recorded in the history of the castle, until it was in-
vested by the forces of Parliament in the Civil War; and a fatal and
surprising weakness was revealed when they cut off the water supply and
forced the garrison to surrender. Afterwards, it was slighted and rendered
uninhabitable.

Caerlaverock Castle
Dumfries

The ruins of Caerlaverock lie 11 kilometres south-south-east of Dumfries, and are a short distance from the Solway Firth, though now protected from it by a woodland screen. A French poem, dating from about
1300, describes the ancient setting: 'And I think you will never see a more
finely situated castle, for on the one side can be seen the Irish Sea, towards the west, and to the north the fair moorland, surrounded by an arm

148

of the sea, so that no creature born can approach it on two sides, without putting himself in danger of the sea. On the south side it is not easy, for there are many places difficult to get through because of woods and marshes and ditches hollowed out by sea where it meets the river'.

The function of the castle may well have been to guard a landing place on the Firth (and an earth embankment leading to the shore supports this supposition). It may have been built c. 1290–1300 as an English bridge-head for the invasion of Scotland by Edward I and, if that is so, it explains why, apart from for topographical reasons, it faced north.

The castle is an equilateral triangle in plan, with a great twin-towered gatehouse at the northern point, and a round tower at each of its other angles. So exact is the geometry that, if the two sides of the triangle are extended, their junction will be found in the true centre of these towers.

There are some indications of an outer courtyard and an arched gate-way to the north of the gatehouse, but if any outer defences existed they have disappeared, and the drawing shows what may be called the castle proper, with its two ditches, the inner one very wide and contained by a pentagonal embankment with a wooden stockade. Some distance to the

Caerlaverock Castle from the north-west, as it might have appeared in the 15th century.

south of the castle are the remains of what is called the 'Old Castle', of uncertain date, which commanded a little harbour.

The drawing shows Caerlaverock as it might have appeared in the 15th century. The earliest existing work belongs to the 13th century—of this date are the western gate tower, portions of adjoining walls and the entire lower courses of the tower on the right, known as Murdoch's Tower. The upper courses of Murdoch's Tower and nearly all the south and east curtains belong to the early 15th century. The other angle tower is 14th-century. A Renaissance fantasy, known as Nithsdale's Apartments, now dominates the interior, but this was only added in the early 17th century.

The plan of the castle has not materially altered since its foundation, and when the rebuilding periods are noted, they may be assumed to indicate destruction wrought by war, for Caerlaverock had a very warlike history. If it is true that the castle was built as an English bridgehead, it must have quickly fallen to the Scots, for in 1300 it was held by them, and Edward I besieged and took it. It remained in English hands until 1312, when the governor announced his allegiance to Robert Bruce: upon his orders it was to be dismantled, rather than left as a potential stronghold for Scotland's enemies. However, the castle was later rebuilt, and fell to the English again in 1347. In 1355 it was recaptured and again demolished by the Scots. By the early 15th century, it had once again been refurbished by the Scots, after a period of desertion, was occupied by the English in Tudor times, recaptured by the Scots, overthrown by the English in 1570, rebuilt by the Scots, and finally besieged and captured by the Covenanters from the forces of King Charles I in 1640. A melancholy tale indeed. In later years it became a romantic ruin, and Sir Walter Scott made it the scene of his *Guy Mannering*, disguising it transparently as Ellengowan Castle.

The fine corbelling at the top of the gate and angle towers fulfilled the same function as the wooden hoardings surmounting the curtain walls: that is, it enabled the defenders to overlook and defeat sapping at the wall foundations.

Bothwell Castle
Strathclyde

Bothwell Castle, standing on the steep bank of the River Clyde where it turns sharply from a westerly to a northerly direction, 13 kilometres from the centre of Glasgow, presents problems of dating and attribution, which make a reconstruction drawing a matter of serious difficulty.

Like the French Coucy or Flint, it is an instance of an isolated round tower dominating the architectural conception, of 13th-century build. However, this great tower or donjon was partly demolished in one of two dismantlings after sieges in 1314 and 1337. When Bothwell was again made defensive in the late 14th century, the demolished work was roughly consolidated, and the south half of the castle courtyard was closed as a rectangle by a straight wall, east and west. In its original form the enclosure was pentagonal in plan, with a twin-towered gatehouse facing north at one of the points of the pentagon, at the junction of two converging curtain walls—but we cannot be sure that this gatehouse or the curtain walls were ever completed!

The history of Bothwell between the late 13th and the late 14th cen-

Bothwell Castle from the south-west, as it might have been completed in the 13th century.

turies is thus a confusion of building, intended building, destruction, demolition and partial rebuilding—an eloquent testimony to the troubles of the times. Because of this confusion, it was finally decided that the re-construction drawing should be of an ideal Bothwell, with perfect donjon, pentagonal courtyard, north gate towers and the south curtain with its high-roofed buildings—one of which, with three tall pointed windows, must have been the chapel. The evidence for these buildings against the south curtain is incontrovertible, and the variation in the shape and size of windows signifies their functions.

A postern gate defended by a portcullis and approached by rock-cut steps has suggested the likelihood of a small turreted gate in the low outer wall, which may well have served a riverside landing place below. The tall round tower to the left of the postern is known as the Prison Tower and is remarkable for its corbelled garde-robes. The square tower to the east was also a latrine tower, and the outflow channel—crossed by a plank bridge—can be seen draining down to the river. The other towers pro-vided domestic accommodation.

The donjon itself was a huge structure, 19.8 metres in diameter, rising above 27.4 metres—circular without, and octagonal within. It was isolated from the courtyard on the inside by a wet ditch 7.6 metres wide, cut out of the rock, and spanned by a wooden bridge ending in a drawbridge. There were four storeys, with wooden floors: a store room and well in the basement; the lord's hall above, to which the drawbridge gave direct access; above that, the retainer's hall, and, on the top floor, the lord's penthouse accommodation or *camera*. A private way led from the *camera* to the Prison Tower and its postern, should the need arise for the lord hurriedly to vacate his castle.

Bothwell was a grand but never a fortunate castle, with a history of destruction. In the Wars of Independence, after the fall of John Balliol, it was held for fourteen months by Stephen de Brampton for King Edward I, before falling to the Scots in 1299. Edward recaptured it in 1301, in less than a month, with a giant siege-engine—a wooden tower or 'belfry' on rollers which was run up against the wall and discharged armed men from its top. This awesome machine was built in Glasgow, and took two days to reach the castle, trundling along a specially made road. Bothwell was then held for the English until their defeat at Bannockburn, when the Scots dismantled it. Again, in 1336 it was restored and occupied by the English; again, a year later, the Scots recaptured it and pulled it down. Then Black Archibald the Grim, third Earl of Douglas acquired it, and after his restoration the castle was inhabited peacefully until the 17th century.

Dirleton Castle
Lothian

Dirleton was another important Scottish castle of sternly romantic appearance, standing on a crag where the land slopes down to the grey waters of the Firth of Forth, 1.5 kilometres away. The building periods extend from the 13th to the 16th centuries.

Basically, the plan is an obtusely angled L-shape, with four part-round towers ranged along the two arms. The courtyard embraced by these two arms on the south and east is closed on the north and west by a curtain wall without towers, raised on the almost vertical crag, which was quarried away to add height to the defences. In the drawing, the south facade of the castle is shown, dominated by the group of three towers at its south-west end. The great round keep is in the foreground, adjoined on its left by a low, square tower carrying a wooden gallery, with a lesser round tower immediately behind. To the right of the entrance is another round tower, and above and behind, the chimneys of the hall and kitchen against the east curtain can be seen.

The ditch, where the fixed bridge crosses it, was 21.3 metres wide. This sloping fixed bridge rose 3.6 metres to a drawbridge fronting the tall and narrow entrance archway—very like that at Caerlaverock—which was constructed between two massive projections shielding the entrance proper, with its double doors and iron portcullis. Two corbelled, snuffer-roofed turrets topped this, and the room between them housed the mechanism for operating the drawbridge. The drawbridge pit (later filled in) can be seen below the entrance.

The keep had an external diameter of 12.2 metres, and was six-sided internally. Both storeys were vaulted, and equipped with fireplaces; the

Dirleton Castle from the south, as it might have appeared in the early 14th century.

upper one was the lord's chamber, and a stair led to a fighting platform on the wall top. At Dirleton there is no breath of the mathematical precision and logic of the Edwardian fortresses, and, as with so many castles, its strength was like that of a muscle-bound heavyweight prizefighter.

The castle was taken by the English after a siege in 1298, and held until 1311. After a partial dismantling by the Scots in the early 14th century, the two round towers on the east curtain were demolished, and replaced by a heavy domestic range in the 14th–15th centuries. Further alterations were carried out in the 16th century, when the Ruthven family owned the castle. In 1650 Dirleton housed 'a nest of Moss-troopers' who preyed upon Cromwell's army, attacking the lines of communication. Cromwellian soldiers besieged and took the place, and demolished the defences.

Kenilworth Castle
Warwickshire

In England an emerging national unity and inner security is discernible in the later history of its castles, whose defences become less important, and private apartments more spacious, until blasted by the rude shock of Civil War. Kenilworth, for much of its existence a royal stronghold, had

153

Kenilworth Castle from the north, as it might have appeared at the time of Queen Elizabeth's visit in 1575.

by the 16th century become an ornate pleasure-house, and the fragility of the later additions made by the Earl of Leicester, for all their splendour, indicates very clearly that the tug-of-war between fortress and residence was nearly over.

The earliest surviving building in stone is the great keep, shown in the centre of the drawing, which dates from between 1155 and 1170. This was a simple rectangle in plan, with a square turret at each angle, and heavily buttressed walls, 4.42 metres thick above the pronounced external batter at their base. It was entered by a staircase to the first floor in the forebuilding attached to its west side. The wide lake that provided the castle with such powerful protection was an artificial creation, formed by damming several small streams—ultimately tributaries of the River Avon—to the south and west.

Kenilworth became a royal fortress in 1199, and King John and his son Henry III energetically developed it. John built the outer curtain wall with towers on all but the waterside—Swan Tower, Lunn's Tower, Mortimer's Tower (at the junction of the dam with the outer bailey), and Gallery Tower defending the further end of the dam—and Henry III completed his work, adding the outwork called The Brays beyond the Gallery Tower. The main entrance to the castle was through the gate with the drum towers in the far distance, and along the causeway over the dam, this causeway being used as a tiltyard in the Middle Ages.

Simon de Montfort's son was besieged here from Easter until Christmas 1266. In the second half of the 14th century the castle passed into the hands of John of Gaunt, who made Kenilworth a palace as well as a fortress. He added most of the domestic buildings in the horseshoe around the inner court: the kitchen and buttery, adjoining the forebuilding of the keep; the great hall (seen end-on in the drawing) with its supporting towers north and south; and the State apartments on the far side. These structures, especially the great hall, were magnificent in scale, with fine fireplaces and lofty windows. The chief rooms were on the first floor, and an external stone staircase led up to them from the inner court.

Kenilworth achieved its peak of fame and glory in the latter half of the 16th century, when it was restored to the Earl of Leicester, whose father had lost possession in Mary's time. Leicester not only added the high block known as Leicester's Buildings, with its large windows and thin walls, to the more southerly prong of the 'horseshoe', but also extensively 'improved' much of John of Gaunt's work. The stone used in the re-building came from Kenilworth Abbey, suppressed in 1539. Leicester also laid out the pleasure garden, built the great gatehouse in the northern curtain and the long barn in the outer court, with its fine timbered upper storey, filled up the inner moat—no longer required for defence—and even modernised the keep by enlarging all its windows. An inventory of 1584 gives a minutely detailed account of the tables, chairs, bedsteads, musical instruments, hangings, carpets, pictures and other furniture which then enriched the castle.

When Queen Elizabeth visited her favourite at Kenilworth in July 1575, there were lavish entertainments: progressing from the Gallery Tower along the causeway, she mingled with pagan gods and antique heroes, while fireworks shot and fizzled in the air. Bearbaiters and Italian acrobats, masquers and musical consorts diverted her during her stay, and she hunted and feasted for 17 days with suitable extravagance. When Leicester died in 1588, the castle declined, and its latter days are a rather sordid tale of disputed inheritance and repossession by the Crown. It was held for Parliament after the battle of Edgehill in 1642, and slighted in 1649, when the north wall of the keep was blown away. In the following year a group of Parliament officers bought the place, and a certain Cromwellian Colonel Hawkesworth had the dam breached, and drained the mere.

Raglan Castle
Gwent

The superb Yellow Tower of Gwent, the outstanding feature at Raglan, was raised between c. 1430–45—on what was probably the motte of the original Norman castle. It was built by William ap Thomas, a soldier of the French Wars, who had married into the family, and who later married the heiress of the Vaughans—both ladies of high birth and great wealth —and it was thus that he celebrated his rise to power and fortune. But times were troubled, and the tower, though finely constructed and com-

Raglan Castle from the east, as it might have appeared at the time of King Charles I's visit in 1645.

fortably appointed, was not purely ostentatious: it was surrounded by a wide wet moat, and could serve as a refuge, if need be, from a mutinous garrison. It was hexagonal in plan, and rose through five storeys: from the kitchen on the ground floor, lit only by combined arrow slits and gunports, through the hall on the first floor, and private room above, to two upper storeys containing bedchambers. Each floor consisted of one large room, and all were connected by a newel stair. The base diameter is 18.3 metres; the walls have a pronounced inward slope.

Access to the tower was originally by means of a drawbridge over the

moat, but ap Thomas's son, William Herbert, first Earl of Pembroke, had this replaced by the arched forebuilding that can be seen in the drawing. Herbert was commercially successful and politically well-connected (he was instrumental in advancing the Yorkist cause, and raising Edward IV to the throne), and his very substantial additions to the castle reflect his wealth and power. He built the two courtyards, parallel in axis, and surrounded by administrative and residential buildings, to north and west of the Yellow Tower. These were divided by the great hall, whose high roof and cupola are visible in the drawing. The great gatehouse (c. 1450–69), also of his building, defended by two portcullises and three strong doors, led directly into the more northerly of the two courts, called the Pitched Stone Court, which served the administrative buildings and kitchen; and this was connected, by a passage through the central great hall and chapel block, to the Fountain Court, so named (according to a visitor to the castle in 1587) from a 'pleasant marble fountain in the midst thereof, called the White Horse'. A splendid grand stair rose from this courtyard to the living apartments which closed it on three sides. None of this is visible in the drawing, but the general richness of the work is evident. Between the great gate and the forebuilding of the tower can be seen the fine windows of the parlour below, and the lord's dining room above.

The low hexagonal wall with corner turrets around the base of the tower was also added by Herbert: the terrace so formed may have mounted light cannon. The Moat Walk belongs to a period of extensive rebuilding in the 16th century, and the niches in its wall, which were adorned with 'several figures of the Roman Emperors in arches of divers varieties of shell-work' are later still. By this date, defence had become very much a secondary consideration: fixed two-arched bridges had replaced the earlier drawbridges to the great gate and the small south gate; the earthwork defending the castle to the south and east had been converted, in part, into a bowling green; and part of it was even excavated away to make easier the passage from the Moat Walk to the outer castle forecourt (left foreground): the resultant gap here, a hopelessly weak point, was spanned by a single-arched bridge.

In the late 16th and early 17th centuries the White Gate in the foreground of the drawing, with its thin curtain-wall, was built as an outer 'protection' for the great gate—a romantic fiction. A further 'protection', the Red Gate, and presumably another wall, was begun further out, but not completed—because the one contingency never expected, that is, war, occurred to prevent it! Raglan is, indeed, a make-believe fortress built in times of relative security, which ironically came to its end through siege and cannonade.

The King was here in 1645; he played bowls upon the smooth green, learned of the surrender of Bristol, and departed. In 1646 began the fatal siege, and Raglan—so far removed from the grim realities of Harlech and Conway, with its orchards and parks and great fishponds 'ornamented with many and divers artificial islands and walks'—suffered from its defensive insufficiencies, as the Marquis of Worcester found to his cost: he 'had to dine in his withdrawing-room to the accompaniment of musket balls coming in through the windows'. Even so, it manfully withstood the spoiling bombardment until the hopelessness of the royal cause made surrender inevitable. A breach had been made in the north wall of the Pitched Stone Court, a 'large and fair compass window' of the parlour knocked out, and the battlements of the Yellow Tower carried away by cannon fire; but this was as nothing compared with the deliberate destruction and plunder that followed. The Herbert estates were forfeited, and Raglan was left in ruins.

Helmsley Castle
North Yorkshire

Helmsley Castle from the south-east, as it might have appeared in the 16th century.

Helmsley Castle, as an example of the effect of changing conditions, is more typical than either Kenilworth or Raglan, which were the products of almost unlimited wealth and power. The keep is c. 1190 and contemporary with the original quadrilateral enclosure of the castle, which was protected by a wide ditch with an outer palisade. The strongly defended barbicans to north and south were added in the mid-13th century: the latter (in the foreground) covered the principal approach, and was

the more elaborate. The walls, gatehouse and corner towers of this outwork were furnished with holes below the battlements for wooden hoardings. The walls spanning the inner ditch were added in the late 13th century, and allowed communication along the wall walks with the main defences. The barbican gatehouse was refaced in the Renaissance manner in the late 16th century.

Stone and timber bridges over the ditch led to the inner gatehouse and the buildings of the inner ward. Immediately to the left of this gatehouse in the drawing are the buttery, bakehouses, pantry and kitchen: these all belong to the late 14th or early 15th centuries. The great hall behind may be slightly earlier.

Behind the great hall a square block called the West Tower can be seen. Its foundations belong with the earliest work in the castle, but in the late 13th century it was largely rebuilt, and square-headed, two-light windows replaced the earlier slits—sure evidence of increasing comfort and se-curity. Towards the end of the 16th century, these in their turn were removed and replaced by new and larger windows. A similar remodelling affected the rest of the buildings lining this curtain at this date, with the insertion of fireplaces, and fine oak panelling, and plaster friezes that still in part survive, bearing the arms of Edward Manners, third Earl of Rut-land, who owned the castle from 1563 to 1587. On the outer face of this block, more light was let into the private apartments by the addition of two oriel windows, and a door was broken through the curtain.

On the opposite side of the courtyard, the building at an angle to the keep was originally a chapel, dedicated in 1246; but, at a later date, a fireplace and chimney were inserted in its east end, indicating a change of use. The small, free-standing structure was the well house. Other less certain foundations survive.

It can be claimed that Helmsley was a concentric castle, but compared with the close-knit, passionate precision of Harlech or Beaumaris, it was a poor thing. The harsh truths of war, which would have imposed a more scientific order, were happily absent for most of its existence, permitting a history of modest improvements. In its degeneracy as a castle it can never have been 'opulent', but was, no doubt, for a long period the scene of a rich and generous social life, far enough from London to have provincial independence, and yet near enough to be fully aware of events, cultural and political.

In 1644, during the Civil War, it was held for the King for three months —its only recorded siege—and slighted when it surrendered. Occupation finally came to an end after the Restoration.

Minster Lovell
Hall
Oxfordshire

The ruins of Minster Lovell Hall stand beside the slow-flowing River Windrush, between Burford and Witney, and present a picture of melan-choly beauty. To the north is the high ground of Wychwood Forest, and to the south the land rises to the Oxford–Gloucester road. At a distance of 0.4 kilometre to the east are the remains of a stone bridge across the river, and it is probable that the main approach to the hall was from this direction.

Just west of the hall is the village of Minster, which takes its name from

Minster Lovell Hall from the south, as it would have appeared before it was dismantled in the 18th century.

the church. 'Lovell', the family name of the lords of the manor, was added in the late 13th century, to distinguish this from the adjacent manor of Little Minster, then held by the Earls of Pembroke. However, there is evidence to suggest that the Lovells owned land here at least as early as the 12th century, and, indeed, that an earlier manor house stood upon this site.

The surviving remains belong, with additions, to the first half of the 15th century and comprise buildings enclosing three sides of a courtyard. The south-west tower, with its ornamental battlements and oriel window, and the buttressed retaining wall along the river's edge, probably date from later in the same century, and the lengths of passage with low roofs on the opposite side of the courtyard may have been added early in the 16th century—otherwise the building is all of a piece. It is worth noting that, except as an architectural feature, the hall did not even maintain the fiction of defensibility, although the old convention of an inner and an outer court is retained.

There was a formal entrance to the main rooms from the gardens of the outer court (on the north side of the central block), but the principal entrance was directly to the inner court, by means of a passage through the east wing, with stables conveniently opening off this on the south side. On the north side of the passage was the kitchen, with extraordinarily thick walls to accommodate ranges. A rough path led along the side of the courtyard from the kitchen to a door in the service passage. Buttery, pantry and bakehouse lay to the right.

The central block was dominated by the great hall, 15.2 metres long, 7.9 metres wide and 12.2 metres high. It had a central fireplace, but, apparently, no corresponding louvre in the roof, and the smoke curling up would have been carried away by a cross-draught from opposite openings at the tops of the end walls. In the drawing, the abnormally high roof of the great hall conceals the chapel, on the first floor behind, above what must have been a fine room lit by three windows.

The small structure jutting out from the hall housed the staircase to the solar—'a sitting room adjacent to the upper end of the hall'. Adjoining this to the left, was the north-west building, with low-ceilinged ground floor rooms, and an upper room entered from the solar. The west wing contained bedchambers, three of the five rooms on the ground floor having fireplaces. There was a well in the north-west corner of the courtyard.

Beyond the hall is the church, which forms a notable feature of the architectural complex of Minster Lovell. There was also a walled outer yard with barns and a splendid pigeon loft, which survives. The whole was set in a great park, a portion of which, under royal licence, was taken from the 'King's forest of Whichewode'.

The last of the Lovell line was Francis, the ninth baron, who may have built the south-west tower and river wall noted above. He served Richard III, fought on the losing side on Bosworth Field, fled to Flanders, and then returned to England in the train of the pretender, Lambert Simnel. He was supposed to have perished in the fighting that took place in that ill-starred rebellion, but there is a legend that he survived and lived long after in a cave or vault. In 1708, when a new chimney was being laid at Minster Lovell, such a vault was apparently found 'in which was the entire skeleton of a man, as having been sitting at a table, which was before him, with a book, paper, pen, etc; in another part of the room lay a cap; all much mouldered and decayed. Which the family and others judged to be this Lord Lovell, whose exit hath hitherto been so uncertain'.

The manor passed through several hands in the centuries after his death, coming at length into the possession of the Coke family. When their great mansion at Holkham was built in the early 18th century, Minster Lovell was abandoned, and dismantled in about 1747.

Deal Castle
Kent

Deal Castle formed part of Henry VIII's coastal fortification scheme, made necessary by the threatening combination of the Papacy with France and Spain. These powers were hostile to the Tudor version of the self-sufficient nationalist state which had come into being largely as a result of Henry's divorce of Catherine of Aragon, and the subsequent movement of England into the Protestant camp.

The defences were concentrated along the south coast and the Thames

Deal Castle from the south, as it might have appeared when newly completed in 1540.

estuary, although other parts of the kingdom, the frontier of Scotland and even the Isle of Man, were not neglected. Deal is one of a trio of forts dominating the Downs, the anchorage formed by the offshore Goodwin Sands, which would have been an ideal place for an invasion from France or the Low Countries. It was built at the height of the crisis, in 1538–40.

That medieval fortresses were inadequate in the face of cannon fire had quickly been recognised, and the artillery fort was devised to answer the new problems of defence. It was scarcely a satisfactory answer, as became obvious before many years had passed, but for a short time these forts must have seemed impregnable in their squat strength.

The great fault in their design lay in the insistence on the rounded form. Round towers were intended to deflect cannon balls and make the direct shattering blow almost an impossibility, but the designers failed to

take into account the devastating play of projectiles ricocheting in a confined space, and also the extravagant cost, in guns and men, of providing adequate flanking fire. This fault was later remedied in the straight-sided bastions of Italian design which were being introduced into England by the middle of the 16th century—of which a further development, influenced by the Dutch school of fortification, can be seen at Tilbury Fort. Again, Deal is of stone throughout, and stone unfortunately shatters under force, causing terrible wounds and damage. This fault, too, was later recognised, and stone walls gave place to earth embankments which could absorb and nullify the shock of cannon balls.

But in spite of the shortcomings, due to its experimental design, Deal was formidable, and that it was untested in war may well be a tribute to its effectiveness as a deterrent.

Built on the very edge of the sea, the castle is surrounded by a flat-bottomed dry moat, 17.1 metres wide, its outer edge strongly revetted in stone. The outer curtain with six semi-circular bastions echoes the revetting of the moat, and the inner curtain, again with six bastions on a higher level, was so arranged that their greatest projections occur at the junctions of the outer bastions. The central round 'keep', with its turret, dominates the whole geometrically exact composition. It is, of course, a version of the concentric fortress, designed to cope with new conditions and new weapons. The only approach was by way of a stone bridge over the moat, equipped with a drawbridge. To reach the keep, the enemy would have been forced to traverse an enclosed courtyard, to a door, one third of the way round the keep from the outer entrance, on the south side, and suffer exposure to fire from the loop-holed walls.

The construction of the keep is interesting, depending as it does on a central hollow pillar containing a well in the basement, and, above that, spiral stairs leading to the first floor and the observation turret. No provision was made for splendour or luxury.

Deal Castle, well prepared for the Armada in 1588, had by 1615 greatly decayed. Later it was repaired, and in the Civil War was the scene of much warlike activity. It was improved for living accommodation in the 18th century, but almost all later accretions were blasted away by a well-aimed bomb in the Second World War, and what remained of them were then removed. Apart from the battlements, which are 18th-century, the castle is today close to its original appearance.

Tilbury Fort
Essex

Tilbury Fort, with the batteries across the river at Gravesend, formed the first line of London's defence through the 18th and first half of the 19th centuries. It owes its survival in its 17th-century form to the fact that, when the Royal Commission on the Defence of the United Kingdom drew up its report in 1860, new forts to accommodate more powerful weapons were recommended to be built further downstream, where forward batteries were already in existence. In the remodelling that followed, drastic alterations to Tilbury were not considered worthwhile, and its old defences were left undisturbed, although heavier guns were mounted. In a reduced role, as a depot and powder magazine, it continued to be garrisoned into the 1920s.

Tilbury Fort, as it might
have appeared from the
south-west, about 1725.

The nucleus of Tilbury Fort was Henry VIII's round-fronted artillery blockhouse on the river's edge. It was one of a group of five such forts erected in 1539 to secure the river approach to London. In later days it was converted into a storehouse. It no longer exists, but seems to have been a simple structure with no architectural grace.

After the Dutch raid of 1667, the need for a more commanding fort on the Thames was recognised, and the design and ordering of construction was given into the hands of Charles II's chief engineer, Sir Bernard de Gomme. De Gomme had accompanied the King in exile, where he would have studied the new systems of bastioned fortification which had become established in the Low Countries. The regular geometry of these forts was straight-edged, with each bastion mounting cannon, and able to give effective flanking and supportive fire. The theory was that the garrison

would retreat line by line as the enemy forced them back, and so fortification in depth returned to fashion. The destructive power of cannon fire also led logically to the abandonment of a central strong point, or keep: instead, there was an open parade ground. Here, in the final stage of its development, we see that the castle has reverted to a barracked camp.

The landward approach was by way of a roughly triangular isthmus—the redan—defended by a redoubt, set in the outer moat on the north side. A short bridge led on to the 'covered-way', the angled outer earthwork with sloping banks, along which troops could be rushed under cover to any threatened point: this corresponded in siting if not in function to the outer curtain of the medieval concentric castle. A further bridge crossed to the ravelin—a fortified island—and thence over the inner moat and across two drawbridges to the Landport Gate. The water level in the moats was regulated by sluices connecting with the river.

The inner 'curtain' consisted of four mutually supporting bastions serving as gun platforms, which projected from four angles of a regular pentagon. The walls were brick-faced, and there was a sentry-box at the salient of each bastion. An obvious irregularity in the plan was the failure to construct a fifth bastion on the river side: the piles for this were driven, but for some reason the work was never carried to completion. Instead, a jetty to the river from the old blockhouse was run out over the site.

To the left of the blockhouse is the Water Gate, the one charming piece of frivolity that de Gomme allowed himself: it is opposite the quay, and is flanked by the chapel and guardhouse. The other buildings in the fort were symmetrically placed officers' and soldiers' barracks, with powder magazines (added in 1716) on either side of the Landport Gate.

Finally, along the river, to east and west were the formidable gun lines. In 1724, according to Daniel Defoe, there were up to 100 guns in all at Tilbury: 'generally all of them carrying from twenty-four to forty-six pound ball, a battery so terrible as well imports the consequence of the place. Besides which there are smaller pieces planted between them, and the bastions and curtains also are planted with guns, so that they must be bold fellows who will venture in the biggest ships the world has heard of, to pass such a battery'.

And yet the fort never saw action, and these great guns were never fired in anger!

Index